SUPERHERO THERAPY
FOR ANXIETY AND TRAUMA

of related interest

Creative Ways to Help Children Manage Anxiety
Ideas and Activities for Working Therapeutically with Worried Children and Their Families
Dr. Fiona Zandt and Dr. Suzanne Barrett
Illustrated by Richy K. Chandler
Foreword by Dr. Karen Cassiday
ISBN 978 1 78775 094 4
eISBN 978 1 78775 095 1

The Creative Toolkit for Working with Grief and Bereavement
A Practitioner's Guide with Activities and Worksheets
Claudia Coenen
Illustrated by Masha Pimas
ISBN 978 1 78775 126 0
eISBN 978 1 78775 147 7

Creative Coping Skills for Teens and Tweens
Activities for Self Care and Emotional Support including Art, Yoga, and Mindfulness
Bonnie Thomas
ISBN 978 1 78592 814 7
eISBN 978 1 78450 888 3

Hell Yeah Self-Care!
A Trauma-Informed Workbook
Alex Iantaffi and Meg-John Barker
ISBN 978 1 78775 245 0
eISBN 978 1 78775 246 7

The CBT Art Workbook for Coping with Anxiety
Jennifer Guest
ISBN 978 1 78775 012 8
eISBN 978 1 78775 013 5

SUPERHERO THERAPY
FOR ANXIETY AND TRAUMA

A Professional Guide with ACT
and CBT-based Activities and
Worksheets for All Ages

Janina Scarlet

Foreword by Dennis Tirch
Illustrated by Dean Rankine

Jessica Kingsley Publishers
London and Philadelphia

First published in Great Britain in 2021 by Jessica Kingsley Publishers
An Hachette Company

1

Front cover image source: Dean Rankine

A CIP catalogue record for this title is available from the
British Library and the Library of Congress

ISBN 978 1 78775 554 3
eISBN 978 1 78775 555 0

Printed and bound in the United States by Integrated Books International

Jessica Kingsley Publishers' policy is to use papers that are natural,
renewable and recyclable products and made from wood grown in
sustainable forests. The logging and manufacturing processes are expected
to conform to the environmental regulations of the country of origin.

Jessica Kingsley Publishers
Carmelite House
50 Victoria Embankment
London EC4Y 0DZ

www.jkp.com

Contents

List of Activities

Acknowledgments

This work would not have been possible without the constant support of my incredible partner, Dustin. Thank you, honey, for all the hugs, for believing in me, and for bringing me coffee at all hours of the day to help my writing. This book would also not be possible without my amazing editor, Jane Evans, whose kind guidance has allowed me to put this work together. I would also like to thank the amazing Dean Rankine for his gorgeous artwork.

Finally, I would like to express my deepest gratitude to everyone who supported me through this process, especially my family—Dustin, Hunter, Eddie, Shaye, Sherry, Rich, Chase, my mom, and my incredible friends—Paxton, Sasha, Shawn, Phil, Jenna, Eugene, Robin, Elina, Alan, and Happy. Andrew McAleer, thank you for always believing in me.

Thank you all for being wonderful.

Foreword

In the age of evidence-based psychotherapy, how do we put Dr. Janina Scarlet's work in context? Even if you are a psychologist who appreciates geek culture, and I am told there are a few of us, the idea of a therapy using superheroes as a central idea could give you pause. Psychotherapy deals with human psychological suffering, coming to terms with experiences such as grief, suicidal thoughts, and life after enduring trauma. What could something as seemingly superficial as superhero lore have to do with such serious matters? As it turns out, there is something potentially liberating in how you relate to symbols of empowerment, compassion, and strength, and Dr. Scarlet has found a key to understanding how to harness this power. By utilizing the metaphor of the hero's journey, and drawing upon archetypes woven into contemporary popular culture, Dr. Scarlet has realized a vision for emotional healing that is at once ancient and post-modern.

Dr. Scarlet's Superhero Therapy does not begin and end in working with symbols and archetypes, however. Wisely, Dr. Scarlet has integrated evidence-based processes and procedures into her approach to psychotherapy, so that her methodology can stand on the shoulders of giants. A range of cognitive and behavioral therapies, with a proven track record in treating anxiety and mood disorders, provide the raw material for Superhero Therapy. Acceptance and commitment therapy (ACT), in particular, forms a solid foundation for much of the work in this book. Beyond integrating psychotherapy techniques, Dr. Scarlet has forged these ideas and methods into something new, even something beautiful. She has given you an archetypal quest item, the sword or grail, if you will, and you, the reader of this book, are challenged to accept the call, and to bring this method into those dark psychological spaces where heroic efforts at alleviating human suffering are needed most.

Some of the most ancient known rituals concerning human emotion and personal transformation, such as the "mystery rites" of Osiris, Attis, Mithras, and Dionysus from thousands of years ago in Central Asia and North Africa, involve a person shifting their state of consciousness to identify with an archetypal and heroic god-form. In the centuries to follow, global wisdom traditions would use symbolic characters in heroic quests as teaching tools to guide people to greater wisdom and personal realization, from the travails of Hanuman and Ram in the *Ramayana* to the tales of the saints of Eastern Orthodox Christianity. From shamanic rites using entheogenic chemicals, to Tibetan esoteric Buddhist visualizations to Sufi chanting or engagement with the devic intelligences elaborated in the Kaballah, archetypal and mythopoetic identification is one of the most consistent and profound techniques we find for emotional growth, across time and cultures. In the world of psychotherapy, the visualization methods we use in compassion-focused therapy (CFT; Gilbert, 2010), self-as-process techniques in ACT, role-playing techniques in experiential therapies, and, of course, Jungian work with archetypes, all draw upon the self-same processes that are the lifeblood of Superhero Therapy.

In secular and capitalist cultures, our access to the evolved, prototypic dimensions of self that myths and archetypes provide can seem elusive. The genius of Dr. Scarlet's work is the way that she finds access to archetypal intelligences hidden in plain sight. By using the metaphors and symbols of superheroes, and the vernacular of popular culture, Dr. Scarlet allows you to leverage deeply embodied social mentalities that have been designed by evolution to serve specific functions. Our protective self, our nurturing self, even our playful self, all become available to us in this way, and we can stimulate the attendant neurobehavioral repertoires that we need to engage with suffering, as we take up the mantle of the hero, the superhero, and practice becoming the version of ourselves that is our heart's deepest wish for what we want to see in the world.

What do superheroes have to do with therapy? Explore your own origin story, identify the latent power that is arising in your heart and mind, face your own shadows and demons, and you may find a surprisingly satisfying answer to this question.

Dennis Tirch, PhD,
Founding Director, The Center for
Compassion Focused Therapy

HOW TO USE THIS BOOK

Dear clinician,

On a daily basis you are serving the people you interact with and helping them find hope even in the darkest of times. I imagine that you have probably seen a gradual increase in posttraumatic stress disorder (PTSD) and anxiety rates in children and adults alike. I certainly have. At the time of a global mental health crisis, we need superheroes. Not just the ones from comic books and television shows, but superheroes like you, who are willing to go to great lengths to meet their clients' needs.

Many people worldwide have sadly never been taught to identify their feelings, and worse, many have been shamed for expressing emotions. As a result, many of the clients that we see feel shame about struggling with a mental health disorder, feel shame about needing help, and feel shame about seeing a mental health professional.

In order to help clients to take the shame and stigma out of mental health, it can be helpful to show them that they are not alone in feeling this way. One way of normalizing and validating the client's experiences is to demonstrate that other people, even superheroes, as well as other courageous heroes have gone through similar experiences as the client has done. This can allow the client to both feel more comfortable sharing their

experiences, as well as to feel more understood by the clinician, establishing trust and rapport. In incorporating examples from popular culture into evidence-based therapy, such as acceptance and commitment therapy (ACT), the ultimate treatment goal would be to assist the client in becoming their own version of a superhero in real life (IRL).

In order to practice Superhero Therapy, you do not have to be an expert in popular culture. In fact, no prior experience is necessary. Your client is the expert in their particular area of interest. You only have to be open minded and curious, acting as a sidekick to your client's hero's quest.

The activities provided in this book will guide you through how to learn about your client's passions and how to incorporate them into treatment. I would recommend that you read through the book once to become familiar with the concepts. Thereafter, feel free to utilize any skills and worksheets as you see fit. You are welcome to photocopy the worksheets from the book or download and print them out from https://library.jkp.com/redeem using the voucher code KQWTKSA at no additional cost. You do not need any additional permission to use these worksheets with your clients or for educational purposes. When using these sheets in educational settings, please be sure to reference the book.

Please remember that just as your client is

the hero of their journey, so are you the hero of yours. Because of you, countless people have found relief and healing. Because of your kindness, many others have felt seen, heard, and supported. And because of you, the world is a kinder, gentler place. And from the bottom of my heart, thank you for being wonderful.

Chapter 1
ORIGIN STORY

For thousands of years, people have used legends and myths to share stories of love, courage, and heroism. In the present day, real life and fictional heroes—such as superheroes and characters from books, television shows, films, and video games—have become a part of the modern myth. In fact, for many individuals, characters from fiction can serve as a kind of *social surrogate* for a friend, family member, and even a romantic partner. Such social surrogates can help individuals feel less isolated and better understood, and can potentially help to raise their self-esteem and a sense of belonging (Derrick, Gabriel, and Hugenberg, 2009). While individuals with a history of trauma might feel less emotionally connected to their classmates, many also report feeling more connected to fictional television characters, which function as their surrogate support systems (Gabriel *et al.*, 2017).

Every person, real and fictional, has an origin story. An origin story is the beginning of the person's journey in which their life takes a different turn (for better or worse). For some individuals, their origin story begins in their childhood; for others it doesn't start until their adolescence or adulthood. Mine started in Ukraine when I was a few months shy of my third birthday. The Chernobyl nuclear accident of 1986 is still considered to be the worst radiation disaster of all time. For days, we were not aware of the severity of the radiation spill, that is until people started getting very sick

and until other countries, primarily Sweden, noticed that the Geiger counters were showing evidence of a radiation leak. My family and I were all affected by acute radiation poisoning, as were most people living in Ukraine and the nearby countries at that time. We received multiple iodine treatments but, in some cases, that was not enough. The radiation poisoning shattered my immune system, making it difficult for my body to fight infections, which meant that I had to go to the hospital even for a simple cold. I would also get frequent blood clots, but my blood wouldn't clot on its own and I sometimes had to go to the emergency room to stop the bleeding.

By far the worst of all the side effects I went through is one that I still experience to this day—my extreme sensitivity to the weather. Whenever the weather changes, especially when the temperature or barometric pressure drops suddenly, I get severe migraines, which sometimes lead to seizures. I remember being about six or seven, lying in a white-walled hospital room wondering if I was going to die. I remember feeling "weak" and "broken" and spending most of my childhood being and feeling sick. I remember reading stories about fantastical heroes who would slay dragons and save the world and wishing so badly to have some kind of magical abilities in order to be able to save not only myself but all the kids in the hospital with me.

I was 12 when my parents and I were able

to move to the United States. We came to the States as refugees after experiencing years of religious persecution for being Jewish. I was starting seventh grade (Year 8 equivalent in the U.K. and First Year equivalent in Scotland).

Do you, by chance, remember being 12?

Most people I ask chuckle or flinch in horror. I often joke that as adults, we should hold some kind of seventh-grade survivors' group therapy. That usually gets a laugh because most of us remember the extremely challenging transition of that age. The social pressures, the changing friendships and social status, and unfortunately for many of us, relentless bullying. Everyone I knew was picked on, and as a girl who did not speak English, a girl who had to miss school whenever the weather changed, and as a girl with a history of radiation exposure, I made an easy target for bullying. People would sometimes ask me if I was contagious, if I was radioactive, and if I glowed in the dark. To the latter, I would sometimes respond with "I am working on it," but the truth is that most of that year I just wanted to die. The worst part of it wasn't the bullying, it wasn't the mean remarks, but rather, it was the fact that I felt completely and utterly alone.

The nightmares made it too difficult to sleep and the flashbacks made it difficult to trust anyone. I didn't know what was happening to me. I didn't know what PTSD was and I didn't know that I was also struggling with depression. During a parent teacher conference, my teacher told my mom that I was a great student but she couldn't understand why I always looked "so sad."

Although I started making friends over time, the feeling of being "an outsider" stayed with me. Even with supportive friends, I felt alone, often believing that I was "a freak" and "too different," and that if people *truly* got to know me, they would reject me and not want

to be my friends. I felt like I was putting on a mask every day, smiling, pretending, and lying about being "fine" every time someone asked me how I was doing.

And then everything changed forever.

I was 16 and working at a movie theater. The theater manager told all of us who were working the shift that day that we were going to have a free midnight screening of *X-Men* later that night. He said that he wanted the entire staff to attend.

I had a lot of reservations. I knew nothing about *X-Men* and wasn't sure I was going to like it. I even considered faking an excuse to get out of it but decided against it.

The tears started at the very beginning. The film opens with Erik Lehnsherr (Magneto) being dragged away from his parents in Auschwitz during the Second World War. Being the grandchild of Ukrainian Holocaust survivors, I was immediately hooked. In trying to get to his parents, Erik bends a metal gate and it becomes clear that he has superpowers. Later known as the X-Men, people with genetic mutations similar to Erik are discriminated against and forced to publicly register as many Jewish people were during the Second World War. Most mutants face bullying and discrimination, sometimes being called "freaks."

I felt like I was watching a movie about my life on the screen. I couldn't stop crying, not from sadness, but because for the first time in my life I felt understood. I saw that I was not alone.

And then I saw Storm. Storm is one of the X-Men who can control the weather. Because the weather always controlled me, it is one of the superpowers I've always wanted. But Storm not only used her powers to control the weather, she used them to save people.

Seeing the effect that *X-Men* had on me made me realize that stories can help people to feel more understood and less alone. It made me rethink my own story and for the first time in my life, instead of thinking of myself as a victim, I thought of myself as a survivor. As the credits were rolling, I sat in my seat, a million thoughts in my mind, realizing for the first time the true power that stories can hold. I realized that fiction could allow us to tell the truth when otherwise talking about difficult experiences might be too painful or even, in some situations, dangerous. I realized that just like me, most people might also have felt alone in their experiences. I realized that people all around us, including the people sitting right next to us on the bus or in the cinema, might also be struggling with the same experiences as what we are going through. And because of this, I realized that stories could help people heal their deepest emotional wounds. It was in that moment that my path became clear to me—I decided to study psychology with an intention to use stories to help people better cope with their painful experiences. I did not realize this at the time, but I was going through posttraumatic growth (PTG), which means finding meaning or a new sense of purpose after one's traumatic experience (Park and Ai, 2006). PTG has been shown to be both a protective resiliency factor against PTSD, as well as a helpful way for individuals with PTSD to recover from it (Park and Ai, 2006; Tedeschi and Calhoun, 1996; Wheeler, 2001).

It was precisely because of *X-Men* that I decided to study psychology. Over the course of my training and clinical practice, I have found that most clients, whether they include children, teenagers, or adults, may have reservations about receiving mental health treatment. Some might understandably believe that a complete stranger will not be able to understand them. They might feel emotionally unsafe and uncomfortable sharing their emotional experiences with someone else,

especially someone they are meeting for the first time. Furthermore, many people might have previously been criticized, shamed, or discouraged for sharing their emotional experiences, while others may have never learned how to understand their emotions.

Interestingly, though perhaps unsurprisingly, I found that many clients, children, and adults alike are far more comfortable discussing the mental health of a fictional character than they are about talking about their own experiences. And by discussing fictional metaphors for the common human experiences, such as anxiety, grief, and trauma, many people appear to feel safer to then self-disclose by sharing the things they have in common with their favorite characters. By creating such fictional parallels of a fictional character's experience with that of a client, the client might have a deeper understanding of their emotional experience, feel more understood by their therapist, and be more willing to engage in therapy-related exercises. This technique of incorporating examples of fictional heroes into therapy to help clients become the heroes of their own journey is called Superhero Therapy. This technique can be implemented into evidence-based therapies, such as acceptance and commitment therapy (ACT), cognitive behavioral therapy (CBT), dialectical behavior therapy (DBT), and others.

Most people assume that Superhero Therapy is intended for work exclusively with children. However, this work is being utilized with clients of all ages and, at least in my case, began as a result of my work with active-duty service members. As a part of my postdoctoral training, I was on a military base where I was working with active-duty Marines who had just returned from the war, most of whom had PTSD. Most service members I was working with had a very difficult time self-disclosing about their experiences on deployment and many shamed themselves for having developed PTSD.

This is an example of a conversation I had with many of my clients:

> Client: I just feel like such a failure.
> Therapist: What makes you say that?
> C: I wanted to be like Superman, you know? Strong.
> T: And now you don't feel that way?
> C: No... I have PTSD.
> T: And what does that mean about you?
> C: It means that I'm weak.
> T: Wow, that's harsh. Let me ask you this, did Superman have any vulnerabilities?
> C: No.
> T: No?
> C: Well, there's Kryptonite...
> T: Right. What is it and what does it do?
> C: Kryptonite is this radioactive material from Krypton, where Superman was born. It takes away his powers and can kill him.
> T: So Kryptonite makes him vulnerable?
> C: Yes.
> T: And does this make him any less of a Superhero?
> C: No, of course not... (Then there's a smile.) Oh, I see what you did there. I get it. Having PTSD doesn't mean I'm not Superman.

The example above shows how often clients might brutally shame themselves for struggling with a mental health disorder, and how bringing up the fact that all heroes struggle can reduce such self-shame in clients. In addition, positive emotional connection with fictional characters can also help clients to be more willing to explore their own emotions and participate in activities that require clients

to face their fears in a therapeutic way (i.e., *exposures* or *committed actions*).

In fact, the willingness to experience discomfort of facing one's fears is one of the greatest therapeutic challenges. Many of the clients who prematurely terminate therapy, do so because they might be struggling with the *willingness* to experience emotional discomfort. In fact, avoidance of any experiences that may bring internal discomfort (i.e., experiential avoidance; Hayes *et al.*, 2006) has been shown to be one of the biggest contributors to the persistence of PTSD and anxiety symptoms, whereas the willingness to experience emotional discomfort has been shown to be one of the largest factors that accounts for improved symptom maintenance. Superhero Therapy can help to encourage clients to face their fears in the same heroic manner as their favorite superheroes do.

Several years ago, I worked with an 8-year-old boy who was deeply traumatized after finding his pet hamster dead in its tank. The boy (let's call him "Mark") picked up the hamster, "Sally," early that morning to give Sally a kiss and a snuggle, as he always did before heading out to school. However, that morning, Sally didn't move. She was cold and stiff and it took Mark a few moments to realize what had happened to his best friend. He dropped her and ran.

Over the next month, Mark struggled with nightmares, he could not sleep in his room alone, he refused to go to the area of the house where Sally died, and refused to go out to the backyard where she was buried. He started having panic attacks and did not feel safe being away from his mum.

When Mark first came in to meet me, he refused to talk about Sally. He shut down and silently cried. After a little while, I asked Mark if it would be all right if we talked about something else for a little bit. He agreed.

I asked if there were any superheroes that he liked and Mark told me that he liked Batman. We spent a good amount of time that session talking about Batman. Mark said that what he liked about Batman was that Batman saved people.

We continued exploring Batman in that session, talking about the villains he faced and what his utility belt looks like. I then told Mark that we would be practicing making our own kind of a utility belt, like Batman's, but that this one would focus on skills and ways that he could learn to face his own fears and defeat his own monsters like Batman does. Mark agreed to try it out.

The next time we met, Mark still struggled a lot. He still had a difficult time sleeping in his room alone and was still avoiding multiple areas of his house, especially the ones that reminded him of Sally. Mark and I then talked about Batman's origin story. Batman (real name Bruce Wayne) was a small child (about 6 to 7 years old), when a mugger killed both of his parents in front of him. Bruce was so upset about this that later, as an adult, he became Batman, a Superhero, in order to make sure that no one else ever lost their family members the way that he did.

Mark knew a lot about Batman and happily told me about Batman's origin story. I also asked him if Batman was ever afraid. Mark wasn't sure until he remembered that Bruce Wayne used to be very scared (phobic, in fact) of bats after falling into a well and getting attacked by them. As Batman, Bruce Wayne then embraced the symbol of a bat as a way of facing his own fears.

Having identified Batman's origin story, I asked Mark if he would be willing to work on identifying his origin story, just like Batman. Mark said that he was willing. With a quivering voice and tears running down his face, he told

me the story of how he found Sally that fateful morning, as well as how much he loved her, and how much he missed her now. He talked about how he was scared to go to the room where she died and to the place where she was buried. That was the first time he told his entire origin story.

I then asked Mark to imagine that Batman found out about what happened to him and came over to help him. I asked Mark what he thought Batman would say and do. Mark thought about it, and then he said that Batman would tell him not to be afraid, that there was no danger, and that he would protect him. He also said that Batman would help him to go to the room where Sally died. Several weeks later I made a house visit to Mark's home and we did just that. He led me to the place where he found Sally and then later, to the place where she was buried. He teared up but he was willing to tell me more about her and share her story with me once more. By this point, he was sleeping in his room by himself on most nights, his nightmares had stopped completely, and after that day, Mark no longer avoided any areas of his house. I couldn't see it with my eyes, but I saw it in my heart—Mark was metaphorically wearing Batman's cape as he was mourning his loss while also being willing to face his pain and his fear.

Whether working with children like Mark, or adolescents, or adults, the therapeutic stance in Superhero Therapy is that the client is the hero of their heroic journey. As therapists, our job is to be the client's sidekick, their biggest fan. Our job is to support the client in following their own life directions and face the monsters that might show up along the way. The overall Superhero Therapy therapeutic model/treatment map looks like this, from origin story through to becoming a superhero IRL (in real life):

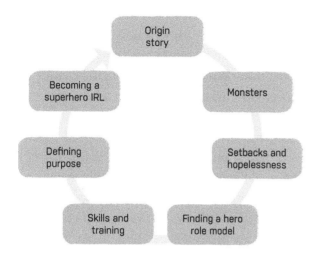

After identifying the client's passions and interests in the first session, the treatment starts with the client's origin story. The subsequent steps include identifying the client's internal monsters, which refers to any unwanted thoughts, feelings, sensations, and memories. Then the client is invited to analyse ways in which their monsters and past experiences have created setbacks for them, often leading to feelings of hopelessness and despair. The client would then identify a heroic role model they can look up to. Subsequently, the client would then learn coping skills, for example, mindfulness, thought challenging or defusion, exposures, or any other related skills (which could be entirely within the therapist's own theoretical orientation, such as CBT, ACT, DBT, or another therapy modality). The client would also be invited to consider their sense of purpose, helping them design their own quest and then learn to take steps to become their own version of a superhero IRL. At the end of the treatment, the client would be invited to rewrite their origin story by incorporating everything they have learned throughout their training. In order to be able to compare the client's origin story to their survivor's story, it is important to hold onto a copy of the client's

initial origin story resulting from the Origin Story activity below.

The activity focuses on helping the client to identify their origin story; the subsequent steps will be discussed in future chapters. The Origin Story activity can allow us to set the stage for our clients—to show them the very beginning of their journey and also to remind them that their origin story does not define them. Every hero has an origin story of their own. Sometimes our origin stories include one horrific event, such as the death of a loved one. Sometimes they include multiple traumatic events, such as years of abuse or neglect. At other times, an origin story can be a seemingly positive change, such as moving to another town or starting a new job. Sometimes even the most positive life events can bring undue stress and feelings of uncertainty and inadequacy.

Exploring our client's origin story can allow them to see the potential of where they would like to take the rest of their story, as well as to receive the support and kindness of a compassionate fictional mentor. Like the well-known "chair exercise," in which a client can talk to an empty chair as if speaking to their younger self or receiving support from their older, wiser self, the origin story invites the client to receive guidance from their favorite heroic role model.

The activities below provide sample scripts that can be used with child and teen/adult clients. They can be carried out as a written reflection (especially for older clients) or as a drawing or a discussion. If the client cannot think of a fictional hero, they can also consider a real-life hero, such as a family member, a teacher, a friend, or anyone who is wise and compassionate. As a default, the client can always consider Batman for this activity.

Origin Story for Teens/Adults

Part 1

Many people go through numerous losses, excruciating physical or emotional pain, and feelings of loneliness and alienation. Just like our favorite superheroes, or real-life heroes, we, too, have an origin story. An origin story can be a memory of a terrible tragedy, an accident, or a moment when we have decided to make different choices.

Take a few moments to consider your own origin story. Do you remember a defining moment that shaped you? Or perhaps it was numerous moments, trying times, and experiences, which at the time felt unbearable.

Part 2

Now take a few moments to identify a personal hero. This is someone you see as a figure of ultimate wisdom and compassion. This could be a real person, such as a grandparent, a teacher, a mentor, a star athlete you admire, a creator, or a historical figure you look up to. Or, it can be a fictional character, such as Batman or Wonder Woman.

If you cannot think of a personal hero, that's perfectly okay. See if you can think of a kind of hero you'd like to have or look up to. What kind of qualities would your hero have?

Part 3

Now, take a few moments to imagine that you have some alone time with your hero. Your hero knows exactly what you have been through, what your origin story is, and how it has shaped you. Your hero is understanding, supportive, and encouraging. Your hero knows exactly what to say to you and what you may need to hear.

What would your hero say to you?

If it is too difficult to think of what your hero may say, no problem. It happens to a lot of people. Take a breath. You can always try this exercise at another time.

Origin Story for Kids

Part 1

Think about your favorite hero, like Batman, Wonder Woman, Harry Potter, or another hero or other fictional character. What do you like about them?

Every superhero has an origin story. Usually, it means that something bad happened to that hero and then the hero later became inspired to use their experience to help other people. Do you know your favorite hero's origin story? What happened to them?

How does this hero help people?

Just like your hero, you also have an origin story. Your origin story is what happened to you. Many kids just like you experience anxiety (or another specific event to the child, such as losing a parent). Often we might not know anyone else that we can talk to about what we feel. So, we might feel alone or somehow different from other kids.

Just like Batman and other heroes, you, too, have an origin story. Your origin story is basically how these fears/symptoms started and how they have been affecting you. Let's talk about/write about your origin story, if that's okay. At any point, if you feel overwhelmed or uncomfortable, we can always stop or take a break.

Part 2

Your hero's story did not end there. In fact, this was just the beginning. Your hero then made a choice to use what happened to them to help other people. They became a protector, a mentor, a superhero.

Let's imagine that your hero is here today. Let's imagine that they come in just to see you, to talk to you about what you are going through. Your hero knows your origin story and knows what you have been through. Perhaps your hero sits down with you and has the kindest message for you. Perhaps something inspiring and supportive. What might your hero say to you?

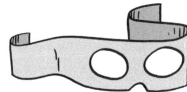

Whenever I talk to clinicians about utilizing Superhero Therapy in treatment, I find that the biggest obstacle most clinicians encounter is that they might feel intimidated by having little to no previous exposure to popular culture. "What if my client talks about a character I know nothing about?" I often hear therapists say. "I don't have time to watch all the *Avengers* movies and read every issue of *Batman*."

The truth is that no matter how knowledgable you are in popular culture, at least one of your clients will bring up a reference you may know nothing about. It happens and it happens a lot, at least to me.

The good news is that you don't have to know everything under the sun about popular culture because *the most important rule of Superhero Therapy is that you do not have to be the expert in popular culture.* Your client is the expert. All you have to be is open minded and curious.

This book is written for clinicians who may or may not know anything about popular culture with tools and questions you can use to find the client's greatest strengths and utilize them to help the client become their own version of a superhero in real life (IRL). So, if you don't know anything about superheroes, Harry Potter, or *Star Wars*, if you've never played *Dungeons & Dragons*, or watched an anime, no worries. This book can be your guide.

Here's an example. A few years ago, I was teaching a class on Geek Culture at Alliant International University, San Diego. The class was designed for doctorate level students to learn clinical skills when working with diverse clients. Although some of the students were familiar with popular culture topics discussed in the classroom, such as *Batman, Avengers,* and *Star Wars,* others did not have much previous experience with them. One of the graduate students, let's call him "Alex," was originally from Nigeria and had no previous experience with American and British popular culture prior to taking this course.

Every week, the graduate students learned about a different fandom (i.e., favorite fan-related franchise, such as *Star Wars,* etc.) and learned how examples from these fandoms can be incorporated into a mental health setting. One of these lectures was about the Avengers. Avengers are superheroes that form a team to fight against various threats to humankind.

The following week, Alex was assigned his first ever clinical case at his practicum site. He had never previously seen a client and it just so happened that his first client was a 16-year-old teenager. Let's call her "Natalie." Natalie had spent most of her life in foster care, bounced from one family to another. She also frequently got into trouble at school and was kicked out of multiple schools for fighting.

When Natalie first saw Alex, saw the color of his skin, saw that he was significantly older than she was, and heard his accent, she folded her arms and said, "I'm not working with you." She likely made an assumption that he couldn't relate to her or understand her. Alex asked Natalie if she would be willing to give him one chance, one session to allow them to get to know each other, and if she still wanted to work with someone else, then Alex would help her ask for another therapist. Natalie agreed.

She was likely expecting him to ask her why she was in trouble with her school again. But that's not what he did. Instead, Alex asked her what kinds of books, movies, or TV shows she liked. After thinking about it, Natalie told him that she really liked the *Ant-Man* movie that she saw. Alex knew nothing about Ant-Man. We never talked about him in our class. So, he simply asked, "Who is Ant-Man?"

Natalie told him that Ant-Man is a superhero who has the ability to shrink himself to the size of an ant, and that he also sometimes fights alongside the Avengers.

Alex said, "Oh, I know a little about the Avengers. There's Hulk, and Captain America, and Black Widow."

Alex described Natalie's reaction as, "She practically lit up. She was smiling. And then she started telling me about Ant-Man's adventures with the Avengers."

Alex then proceeded to ask her, "What is it that you like about Ant-Man?"

Natalie thought about it and said, "I like that he can make himself really small, you know, the size of an ant. I like that he can almost disappear if he wants to."

Alex asked her if she ever wished she could disappear, to which Natalie replied, "Yeah. Like all the time. I feel like everyone is always staring at me. Waiting for me to screw up." Alex asked her about some of the times she felt this way. The two continued talking for the rest of the session, at the end of which, Natalie requested to only work with Alex.

Alex knew very little about popular culture; he had never heard of Ant-Man, and was new to being a clinician. But he was willing to be open and curious about his client's passions, understanding them to be important for her self-expression. Through the lens of the Ant-Man metaphor, Alex was able to let Natalie feel more heard and supported than she had previously, even with very experienced therapists.

Our clients' interests and passions are not just their hobbies. They are a part of them, and if that part is ignored, the client will likely feel misunderstood, or believe that they cannot be open about who they are. But if their interests are welcomed and explored in therapy, clients are more likely to open up, building stronger rapport and willingness to comply with therapy-related activities. What might seem like a "waste of time" to some, in terms of spending some time to explore the client's passion for a particular book series, movie, TV show, game, or other activity such as cosplay (i.e., dressing up in costumes related to one's fandom) might actually be an investment into a stronger therapy alliance and adherence to treatment. The following gives some sample questions you can ask your clients to learn about their interests. For small children, or for clients with developmental or learning disabilities, you can use the worksheet as a prompt to ask them any relevant questions and write in the answers yourself. Not all the questions have to be answered.

Questions to Gauge a Client's Interests

(ALL AGES)

1. What kinds of movies, books, or TV shows do you like?

   _____

   _____

   _____

   _____

2. What do you like about your favorite movie/book/TV show?

   _____

   _____

   _____

   _____

3. What is it about?

   _____

   _____

   _____

   _____

4. Who is your favorite character?

   _____

   _____

   _____

   _____

5. What do you like about them?

   _____

   _____

   _____

   _____

6. Have you ever had situations in which you felt this way or wanted to feel this way (e.g., empowered, protective, etc.)?

_____

_____

_____

_____

7. What kinds of games (video games, card games, role-playing games) do you like to play?

_____

_____

_____

_____

8. How is your favorite game played?

_____

_____

_____

_____

9. What is your character like in this game?

_____

_____

_____

_____

10. What did you like about playing as this kind of character?

_____

_____

_____

_____

11. Who do you typically play with?

_____

_____

_____

12. Do you like the people you play with (if multiplayer game)?

_____

_____

_____

_____

13. What do you like about the other players?

_____

_____

_____

_____

14. Do you ever get this kind of benefit (e.g., time with friends, feeling of empowerment, feeling accomplished) in other situations? If so, which ones?

_____

_____

_____

_____

15. What are some of the situations in which you wish you could experience the same benefit that you receive from this game/activity (e.g., friendship, feeling accomplished)?

_____

_____

_____

_____

Whether you are an expert in popular culture, or brand new to it, please know that it is perfectly okay to feel nervous about implementing new skills into treatment. As mental health professionals, we have a lot of pressure on us. The clients you are working with might be running out of hope, might be thinking about giving up, and might have a lifetime worth of suffering. In my experience, these questions might remind the client of why life matters, of life's joys, and what makes them feel alive.

One of my friends and colleagues, Travis, is a Marine Corps Veteran and a social worker. At the time, Travis was working as a peer-support specialist, helping other veterans with PTSD to manage mental health struggles. One day, Travis was leaving a group he was facilitating when he saw a veteran he had not seen before in the waiting room. This veteran, let's call him "Mike," was not Travis's client but Travis decided to introduce himself. Travis noticed that Mike was wearing a hockey hat. Being an avid hockey fan himself, Travis asked Mike about his favorite team and the two spent about 10 minutes talking about hockey. They talked about their favorite teams, ragged on each other, and talked about their favorite hockey moments. Mike grew up playing on frozen lakes and reminisced about being a child. Travis eventually asked Mike why he came in; he was seeing his new counselor and did not know what to expect. Travis disclosed that he was also a veteran with PTSD and that counseling helped him to better manage his symptoms. He told Mike to let him know if there was anything he could do for him or help him understand from a veteran's perspective.

The following week, Travis was leaving the same group and saw Mike in the waiting room again. He waved hello and was about to keep walking when Mike asked him to "wait up." Mike came up to Travis and thanked him for talking to him the week prior. He disclosed that he was intending to go home and kill himself that night but that talking about hockey reminded him how passionate he was about it. Talking to Travis allowed him to feel that he wasn't alone. The connection that he felt with Travis in being able to talk about his favorite sport possibly did as much, if not more, to help him that day as a therapy intervention. And this connection allowed him to be more willing to try therapy and to follow through with his appointments and therapy-related activities.

The truth is that you are in this profession for a reason. You save lives on a daily basis. You probably recall the origin story activity we talked about earlier, regarding receiving support from a heroic role model. For many of your clients, that heroic role model is you. Many of them probably have imaginary conversations with you, confiding in you, listening to your guidance. There are probably multiple people who are alive today because of something kind that you did and said. Most of them will never tell you that but I wanted you to know—*you* change lives on a daily basis. In this therapy quest, *you* are the Chosen One. You make a difference. So, from the bottom of my heart, thank you for being wonderful.

Chapter 2

IDENTIFYING MONSTERS

MIND DUNGEONS AND EMOTION DRAGONS

Once the client is able to understand their origin story, the next step is to help them to identify any monsters that stand in their way. Monsters are any of the client's unwanted thoughts, feelings, sensations, and memories. Although monsters (e.g., anxiety) often *feel* dangerous, they are not actually harmful. Monsters are not the perpetrators of abuse; they are the result of it. This means that monsters are sometimes the client's own defence mechanisms, or ways that they have learned to keep themselves safe.

For example, a client who experienced bullying and emotional abuse might develop depression, as well as social anxiety. This client might also develop thoughts such as, "I am worthless," and "If I get close to someone, I will be rejected and hurt." In some ways, these thoughts and emotions might be protective in that they might be keeping the individual safe. The thoughts might, for example, lead the client to disengage from social interactions, potentially preventing them from experiencing such painful events again in the future.

However, in the long term, there might be a serious cost if the individual were to continue to abide by these thoughts.

According to acceptance and commitment therapy (ACT), it is not the painful thoughts and feelings that are the problem, it is our unwillingness to face them (Hayes, 2019). The more we try to escape an uncomfortable emotion such as anxiety (i.e., engaging in *experiential avoidance*) the more we are likely to feel it. For instance, if someone who has a fear of heights was to be told that they are not allowed to feel anxious when standing on a roof of a very tall building, that person would likely have a panic attack. However, if that individual is allowed to experience their anxiety, they might be more willing to *feel* anxious and nevertheless remain in the situation that makes them anxious.

The next activity gives an experiential example that I often use with clients to demonstrate this point. With younger children it would be preferable to talk about their experiences rather than asking them to write.

The Pink Unicorn

(ALL AGES)

Take a look at this unicorn. Imagine that you were actually looking at a unicorn like it, perhaps a pink unicorn.

Now, close your eyes for a moment and imagine the pink unicorn. Can you visualize it?

Now, keeping your eyes closed, I'm going to ask you to completely erase that pink unicorn from your mind and memory for the next 30 seconds. So, do not picture the pink unicorn, do not even think of the words "pink" or "unicorn" at all.

Ready? Go.

After 30 seconds, please open your eyes.

What was this experience like?

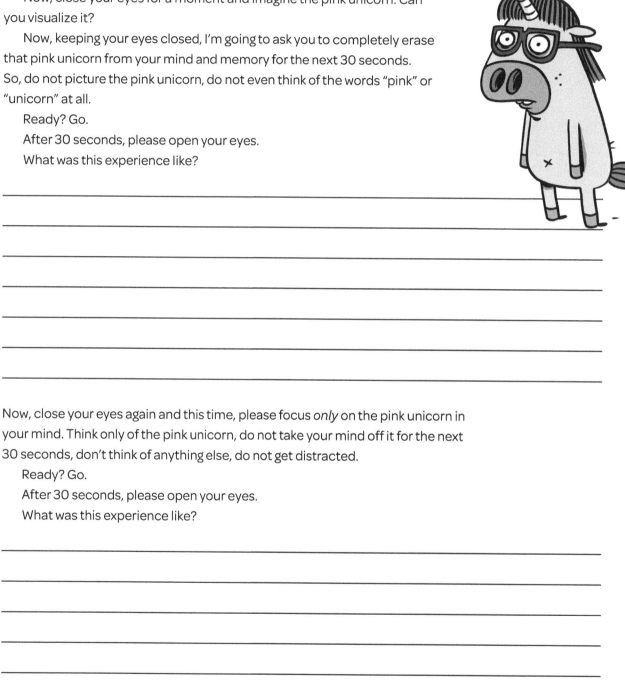

_____

_____

_____

_____

_____

_____

Now, close your eyes again and this time, please focus *only* on the pink unicorn in your mind. Think only of the pink unicorn, do not take your mind off it for the next 30 seconds, don't think of anything else, do not get distracted.

Ready? Go.

After 30 seconds, please open your eyes.

What was this experience like?

_____

_____

_____

_____

_____

_____

Emotional suppression

Although not everyone will experience the same reactions, the vast majority of people will report that they were unable to completely block out the pink unicorn from their minds, and that even as they tried to focus on something else, the image or the thoughts of the pink unicorn would pop back into their mind. Most people also report that when they purposely try to focus only on the pink unicorn, they are unable to maintain their focus on it and the image eventually fades. Similar experiences can be observed with our emotions. Purposely trying to suppress emotions can lead to a more intense version of that emotion. If suppressed, emotions can multiply and grow into an even more extreme form of the initial emotion.

The following worksheets can be used to discuss the unhealthy effects of emotional suppression with clients.

Suppressed Emotions and Their Reactions

(AGES 11 AND UP)

A lot of times, when painful and uncomfortable feelings come up, we might feel the urge to run away from that emotion, to avoid it. However, unprocessed emotions can make us feel worse in the long term.

Feelings are not meant to be suppressed, they are meant to be *felt,* that is why they are called *feelings.* If suppressed, emotions can multiply and grow into an even more extreme form of the initial emotions. For example, suppressed or unprocessed grief can lead to depression, and in some cases, panic attacks. Here are some examples of initially painful emotions and what they can grow into if the initial emotions are not addressed.

Initial emotion	Emotion resulting from suppression
Grief; sadness	Depression; panic; anger
Anxiety; fear	Panic; phobia; irritability
Loneliness; sadness	Depression; irritability
Self-doubt; embarrassment	Shame; depression
Annoyance; frustration	Anger; rage

Have you experienced any of these emotions?

_____

_____

What are some of the examples of situations in which you experienced these emotions?

_____

_____

_____

_____

_____

_____

_____

_____

All of these emotions—sadness, anger, or fear, are important and useful because they are telling us what we need. Everyone feels these emotions, even superheroes and other fictional characters.

Can you think of an example when a fictional hero you like might have felt scared, angry, or sad? What was going on for this character?

_____

_____

_____

_____

_____

What do you think this character needed at the time? For example, support, protection, or maybe, a friend?

_____

_____

_____

_____

_____

How would this hero feel if they never ever received this kind of support?

_____

_____

_____

_____

_____

Just like the character, just like your favorite hero, you too deserve to be supported when you feel this way. As you can see, these emotions are not actually dangerous themselves, they provide us with important information—they let us know what we need, so that just like our favorite heroes, we too can get all the support that we need to get us through it.

Hiding from Our Emotions

A lot of times, when we feel a strong emotion, like when we feel sad or afraid, we might want to do everything possible not to feel that way. It makes sense, and sometimes that's the right thing to do. But sometimes when we try to hide from all our emotions, we might actually feel worse over time. For example, if we feel scared and we never learn to face our fears, then we might become even more scared over time.

Let's think of some of the emotions that you have experienced before. Can you think of a time you ever felt scared before? What was going on then?

_____

_____

_____

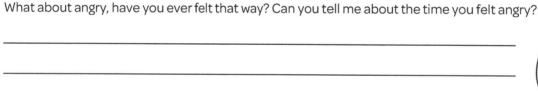

How about the feeling of sadness? Have you ever felt sad? What was going on then?

_____

_____

_____

What about angry, have you ever felt that way? Can you tell me about the time you felt angry?

_____

_____

_____

All of these emotions—sadness, anger, or fear—are important and useful because they are telling us what we need. Everyone feels these emotions, even superheroes and other fictional characters.

Can you think of an example when a fictional hero you like might have felt scared, angry, or sad? What was going on for this character?

_____

_____

_____

_____

_____

☆

What do you think this character needed at the time? For example, support, protection, or maybe, a friend?

_____

_____

_____

_____

_____

_____

_____

_____

How would this hero feel if they never received this kind of support?

_____

_____

_____

_____

_____

_____

_____

_____

_____

Just like the character, just like your favorite hero, you too deserve to be supported when you feel this way. As you can see, these emotions are not actually dangerous themselves, they provide us with important information—they let us know what we need, so that just like our favorite heroes, we too can get all the support that we need to get us through it.

Understanding emotional suppression

Understanding how situations might cause certain emotional reactions can help clients to be able to identify such emotions in these situations in the future. These discussions can also help to normalize the client's experience, potentially reducing any shame or stigma that they might be carrying about experiencing these emotions.

Another activity to help the client understand how emotion avoidance and suppression can backfire is Fizzy Drink.

Fizzy Drink

Our emotions are kind of like pressure in a fizzy drink. When we get shaken up, the pressure builds and that pressure has to go somewhere. What happens to our emotions if we keep suppressing them versus releasing them slowly over time? Let's think of what happens with a fizzy drink.

1. Have you ever had a fizzy drink? If so, what kind?

_____

_____

_____

2. Have you ever shaken the fizzy drink bottle before opening it? What happens when you open the bottle after it's been shaken?

_____

_____

_____

_____

3. Why do you think it happens that way?

_____

_____

_____

_____

4. What happens if you slowly open the bottle over time?

_____

_____

_____

_____

A game of tag with your emotions

The intention of this exercise is to demonstrate that emotions are not meant to be suppressed. I often talk about emotions as our inner magic and explain that magic is meant to be expressed, not suppressed—just ask Elsa.

The idea behind these activities is to assist the client in understanding that rather than suppressing their internal monsters, it can be more beneficial to acknowledge them, name them, and even get to know them. "Name it and you tame it" goes a famous phrase regarding acknowledging and experiencing our emotions (Neff and Germer, 2018), and it seems to be accurate. As mentioned above, when people engage in experiential avoidance, they are more likely to experience more of the very emotion that we are trying to run away from (Hayes, 2019). However, what happens if instead of them running *away* from their emotion, they run *toward* it?

I have a cat, named Vader, with whom I like to play a game of tag. I chase Vader around until he runs into a corner and has nowhere to run. At this point, Vader turns around and looks at me and I start running away, with Vader chasing me around until I run into a corner, at which point I turn around and then start chasing him. This game of tag demonstrates that our clients can keep running until they can't run any more, but at some point they need to turn around and face their anxiety, grief, trauma, and other emotions or memories. Like a game of tag, our clients might need to turn around and not only face their emotions, but perhaps even purposely get to know them. One strategy for doing that is the Name Your Monster activity.

Name Your Monster for Teens/Adults

Many people spend a large portion of their lives running away from their monsters precisely because they believe them to be dangerous. But what if we first got to know them? There is a famous expression in psychology, "Name it and you tame it." This means that sometimes by naming our monsters and getting to know them, we can make them less intimidating.

Do you know who your own monsters are? Here are examples of what some people might imagine their monsters look like:

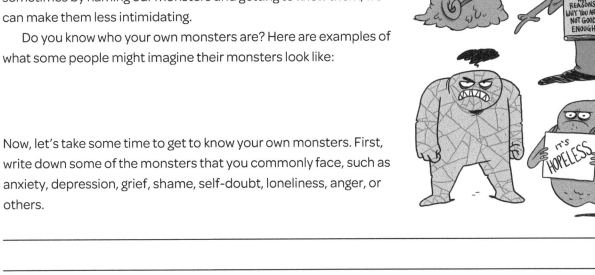

Now, let's take some time to get to know your own monsters. First, write down some of the monsters that you commonly face, such as anxiety, depression, grief, shame, self-doubt, loneliness, anger, or others.

_____

_____

_____

Next, take some time to draw them and color them in (seriously, try it—it's fun).

Name Your Monster for Kids

Many people spend a lot of their lives running away from their emotions monsters because they think that these feelings are dangerous. But our feelings are not dangerous. In fact, they can even be helpful, because they let us know what we need. For example, when we feel sad, it might mean that we need support, and when we feel scared, it might mean that we need safety and protection.

There is a famous saying, "Name it and you tame it." This means that sometimes by naming our monsters and getting to know them, we can make them less scary.

Do you know who your own monsters are? Here are examples of how some people might imagine their monsters look:

Now, let's take some time to get to know your own monsters. Draw some of the monsters that you commonly face, such as anxiety, sadness, shame, self-doubt, loneliness, anger, or others. Please draw them and color them in.

Knowing and understanding monsters

Getting to know our own typically unwanted experiences, such as emotions, sensations, and memories, can make them more manageable and less overwhelming. In fact, psychologists Kristen Neff and Chris Germer discuss the idea of "Feel it and you heal it" in their book on mindful self-compassion (Neff and Germer, 2018). I have experienced this on a very personal level. Because of my past history of Chernobyl radiation exposure, I am extremely sensitive to weather changes. I often experience severe migraines, which sometimes result in seizures. Although I have become comfortable sharing the physiological toll weather changes have on my body, I have never shared the psychological effects of weather changes. Like many other people with seasonal affective disorder (SAD), when the weather changes I experience severe depression, sometimes alongside anxiety and irritability. Usually this is due to the sudden drops in serotonin levels in my body that some people experience with seasonal and weather changes.

What I have noticed about myself is that I could be functioning perfectly well one day and be completely overwhelmed with debilitating depression and drowning anxiety the next just because the weather is changing. Living in sunny California has allowed me a much-needed refuge from the kinds of emotional exhaustion I experienced when living in New York. Still, no matter how many years I have been dealing with weather-related mental and physical distress, I frequently find myself completely surprised and unprepared when a new attack comes. It is as if my body goes through a form of amnesia that does not allow the memory of the emotional pain to remain because each time I go through it, I feel surprised at the depth and extent of it.

I have been used to physical pain. I can function perfectly well with a migraine and have given multiple talks and workshops while in a 9/10 pain. However, the emotional pain has been much harder to work with. In the past, I used to try to manage my emotional struggles with chocolate and TV shows. And although I still occasionally have chocolate and still love to sit down and watch an episode or two (or three) of my favorite show, my relationship with these coping mechanisms has changed. I used to engage in these behaviors because I wanted not to feel bad. I now engage in them *because* I don't feel well, as a way of caring for myself. I also found that I engage in these behaviors less now than I used to because instead of utilizing chocolate and TV shows to run away from my painful exemptions, I now face my internal experiences. I have learned that by allowing myself to feel depressed, anxious, and irritable, and treating it as a sacred space for these emotions, I am able to reduce my own suffering. Don't get me wrong, my depression is still there, as is my migraine. Those elements will forever accompany weather changes in my life. What has changed, however, is that I've become more welcoming of these experiences, treating them as expected guests, making emotional space for them and even arranging my schedule in such a way that I am able to honor them.

Here's an activity I've used in helping clients understand what monsters can look like when they are avoiding them versus when they are facing them.

Monster Sizes for Teens/Adults

(AGES 13 AND UP)

The more we avoid our internal monsters, the bigger they appear. The more we face them and get to know them, the less intimidating they appear.

1. In the box below, draw one or two of your monsters and yourself running or facing away from them (feel free to use stick figures). Please make the monsters significantly bigger than you.

This is what happens when we are trying to avoid or run away from our emotions.

2. Now, draw yourself facing your monsters. Please make the monsters the same size as you.

This is what happens when we face our emotions.

3. Now, draw yourself talking to your monsters, making the monsters smaller than you.

This is what happens when we engage with our emotions.

Monster Sizes for Kids

The more we avoid our feelings, the stronger we might feel them. For example, the more we try not to laugh, the more likely we might be to start laughing. Also, the more we try not to feel sad, the more likely we are to feel even sadder. However, the more we allow ourselves to feel our feelings, the less intense they become.

1. In the box below, draw yourself running away or facing away from your feelings (feel free to use stick figures). You can draw your feelings as one or two monsters that are running after you. Please draw the monsters to be much bigger than you.

This is what happens when we are trying to avoid or run away from our feelings.

2. Now, draw yourself facing your monsters making the monsters the same size as you.

This is what happens when we notice our feelings.

3. Now, draw yourself talking to your monsters or maybe even playing ball with them. Make the monsters smaller than you.

This is what happens when we can feel our feelings.

Grief

One of the emotional experiences commonly avoided by many clients is grief. In fact, experiential avoidance related to grief is associated with complicated grief, depression, anxiety, and other mental health struggles (Eisma *et al.*, 2013). Interestingly, fictional characters can be utilized to help people understand and process their grief experiences (Markell and Markell, 2013). I will never forget my first fictional death. I was 9 years old. My mother was working late and my father was making mashed potatoes for dinner. I was reading my favorite short story collection book, *The Memoirs of Sherlock Holmes.* The story I started that night had an ominous title, "The Final Problem."

At this point in my life, Sherlock Holmes was a personal hero of mine, someone I looked up to, someone who became a surrogate friend and teacher in my eyes. As I flipped through the pages, I started getting a bad feeling that something was going to happen to my favorite character. I could somewhat hear my father calling me to supper but I had to finish the story first. I *had to* know what happened to him. By the time I got to the end, I was sobbing.

My father ran into my room. "What happened?" he asked.

"Sherlock died," I managed to say between the sobs.

"Oh...um...well...the potatoes are getting cold," my father said and walked out of the room.

I couldn't eat that night. I was devastated. My father didn't understand why and to be honest, I didn't either. After all, Sherlock was just a fictional character, right? Then why did I care?

It took me a few years to reflect on this experience until I finally figured out why a fictional character's death affected me the way that it did. A few years prior to this incident, my grandmother on my father's side had passed away. It was the first time I had ever seen my father cry. My heart broke for him and I swore to myself that day that I would focus on supporting him through his loss and that he would never see me crying over my grandmother's passing. However, reading about the death of my favorite character and reading about the grief that his best friend, Dr. John Watson, experienced gave me the permission to honor and process my own grief, which was over 2 years overdue.

Although many of our clients experience grief, few actually acknowledge it and very few know how to talk about it. Incorporating examples from popular culture, as well as asking clients to generate their own examples of grief in pop culture, can de-stigmatize the experience of grief and normalize it.

Here is a worksheet that can be used when working with clients who struggle with grief.

Grief

Grief is a common experience; many people lose people they care about. That is why there are so many books, movies, TV shows, and video games that show someone going through grief. Characters such as Harry Potter, Batman, Wonder Woman, and the Winchester brothers (from *Supernatural*) have all lost people they loved and cared about. And they all needed to understand their grief in order to become the heroes that they did.

Let's try the following exercise to begin to process your own grief with the help of your favorite characters.

1. Name a fictional character who had lost someone.

    _____

    _____

    _____

    _____

    _____

    _____

    _____

    _____

2. What happened to them?

    _____

    _____

    _____

    _____

    _____

    _____

    _____

    _____

    _____

☆

3. If you knew that this character was grieving/feeling very sad, what would you say to them if you could?

_____

_____

_____

_____

_____

_____

_____

_____

_____

_____

_____

4. If that character could talk to you to support you, what would that character say to you?

_____

_____

_____

_____

_____

_____

_____

_____

_____

_____

_____

Finding social support through fictional characters

After experiencing grief or a traumatic event, some individuals might be more likely to turn to favorite TV shows than real-life individuals, as they are seeking a sense of personal connection (Gabriel *et al.*, 2017). One of the reasons why people who have undergone trauma or grief might shy away from communicating their emotions to people they know is for fear that they will not be supported or understood, or that doing so would make them look "weak." Understanding how various characters cope with grief and trauma can help the client to consider opening up to others and focus on finding a sense of connection with other people.

The following worksheets are designed to assist clients with this practice. When working with young children, as well as clients with developmental or learning disabilities, you can write the answers yourself while assisting the client with the questions for discussion.

"I Am Not Alone" for Teens/Adults

(AGES 13 AND UP)

Everyone goes through grief and anxiety, and many people experience depression or trauma at some point in life. As painful as these experiences might be, the most challenging part about them is feeling as if we are going through them alone. The truth is that you are not alone in feeling this way. Just about every person and just about every hero, real or fictional, has experienced something like this at some point or another. Let's see if we can identify how heroes have coped with feeling alone.

For example, Harry Potter is often shamed by his relatives for being magical. He is sometimes bullied by his classmates, and on occasion struggles with feeling like he doesn't fit in, like no one can understand him. Let's see if we can find other examples.

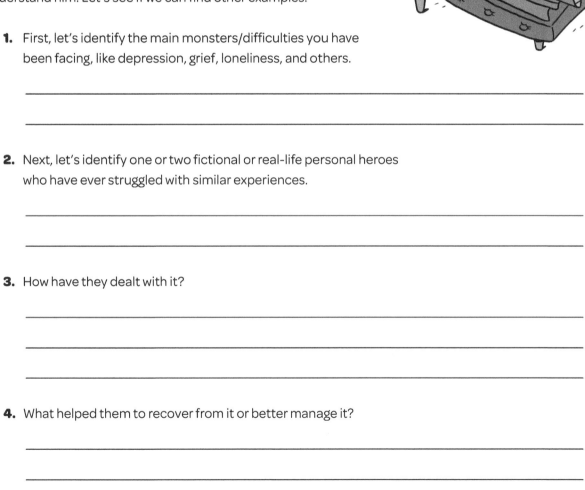

1. First, let's identify the main monsters/difficulties you have been facing, like depression, grief, loneliness, and others.

    _____

    _____

2. Next, let's identify one or two fictional or real-life personal heroes who have ever struggled with similar experiences.

    _____

    _____

3. How have they dealt with it?

    _____

    _____

    _____

4. What helped them to recover from it or better manage it?

    _____

    _____

    _____

"I Am Not Alone" for Kids

(AGES 7–12)

Everyone feels sad, angry, or scared at some point in life. As hard as these feelings might be, the most difficult part is going through them alone.

The truth is that you are not alone in feeling this way. Just about every person and just about every superhero has felt what you are feeling at some point or another.

Let's see if we can think about how other heroes cope with feeling alone.

For example, Harry Potter is often shamed by his relatives for being magical. He is sometimes bullied by his classmates, and sometimes feels like he doesn't fit in, like no one can understand him. Let's see if we can find other examples.

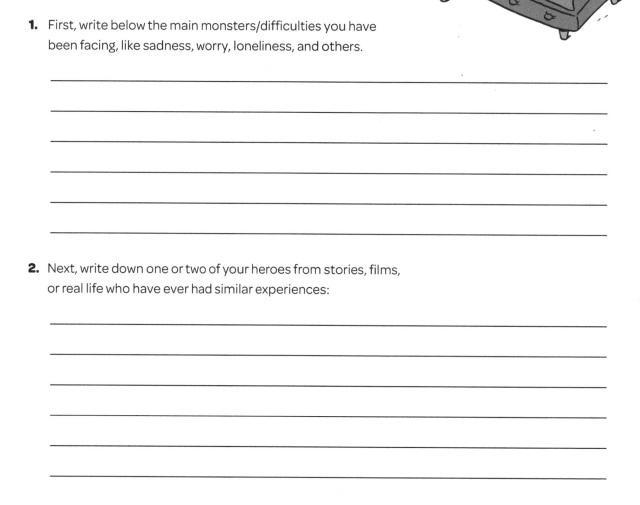

1. First, write below the main monsters/difficulties you have been facing, like sadness, worry, loneliness, and others.

_____

_____

_____

_____

_____

_____

2. Next, write down one or two of your heroes from stories, films, or real life who have ever had similar experiences:

_____

_____

_____

_____

_____

_____

3. How have these heroes dealt with feeling this way? Did these heroes talk to their friends? Did they continue their hero mission?

_____

_____

_____

_____

_____

_____

_____

4. What helped them to feel better over time?

_____

_____

_____

_____

_____

_____

_____

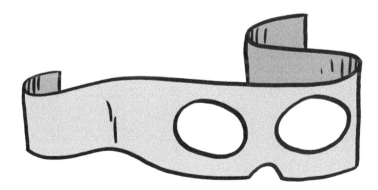

☆

Clients are not the only ones who fall into the trap of thinking that they are alone or that they will appear "weak" if they are struggling. Much like the many people you help on a daily basis, you too are allowed to have a difficult day. You too are allowed to go through a hard time. And you too are allowed to turn to your own personal heroes for comfort. Please know that just like the many heroes your clients turn to in their time of need, they are also turning to you. Your work matters. You matter. And you are making a difference. From the bottom of my heart, thank you so much for everything you are doing to make this world a better place.

Chapter 3

OVERCOMING SETBACKS

As therapists, our job is to be the client's sidekick, their biggest fan. Our job is to support the client in following their own life directions and face the monsters that might show up along the way. A number of different internal and external aspects can pose as obstacles in the client's life. Perceived internal obstacles include the client's thoughts, emotions, sensations (e.g., pain), and memories, whereas external obstacles include the client's environment (e.g., abuse or domestic violence), as well as external situations, including the client's lack of resources, death of a loved one, sudden illness, loss of a job or a home, or a global pandemic.

As if all of these obstacles were already not challenging enough, many clients, kids, and adults alike might be further affected by the erroneous notion that they *should not* feel the way they do and that they *will never be able to overcome these obstacles*. In CBT terms, we would possibly call these thoughts *automatic thoughts* or *cognitive distortions*. Hence, an individual would be guided through thought challenging (i.e., evidence testing) to determine the accuracy of their beliefs (McGrath and Repetti, 2002).

In ACT terms, we could refer to clients' preoccupation with their thoughts as a form of *cognitive fusion*. When individuals are fused with their thoughts, such as "I am worthless," it means that they might be struggling to differentiate between the experience of having

such a thought and a fact. Hence, cognitive defusion serves as a way of changing the person's relationship with a particular thought (for example, through repetition of the word or a sentence, which can lead to a lesser emotional activation and the believability of the original thought; Masuda *et al.*, 2010).

Many clients, both kids and adults alike, can be held back by their thoughts, often assuming that because they *believe* they are incapable of facing their obstacles, it is automatically true. Such thoughts can become an internal obstacle for the client, sometimes causing them to further create external obstacles for themselves. For example, a client who believes they are worthless and incapable might then engage in avoidance behaviors, which could become a form of self-fulfilling prophecy for the client—creating the very outcome they are trying to avoid.

Holding onto rigid beliefs, such as "I should never make mistakes" or "I should never do anything that makes me feel uncomfortable or insecure," is a form of *psychological inflexibility*, in which the individual attempts to control their internal states so as to reduce feeling "bad" and maximize feeling "good." Unfortunately, the very attempts to control one's internal state and the unwillingness to experience anything that might produce internal discomfort can actually further that individual's suffering (Hayes *et al.*, 2006). Thoughts and emotions are an all-or-none packaged deal, which means that the attempts to suppress thoughts and emotions that make someone uncomfortable, such as "If I try this, I will fail," can lead to emotional numbness, depression, and lowered self-efficacy.

On the other hand, increasing psychological flexibility can help the client to remove one of the biggest obstacles they might face (Hayes, 2019) on their heroic journey of life. A recent study demonstrated that Superhero Therapy can be utilized to help college students to significantly increase their psychological flexibility, courage, and self-compassion (Prasad, Scarlet, and Prasadam, unpublished) after ten sessions.

Since psychological inflexibility is often one of the clients' biggest obstacles, one of the goals of ACT (and Superhero Therapy) is to assist the client with developing psychological flexibility. Psychological flexibility refers to the client learning to be mindful of and willing to experience their internal experiences (i.e., thoughts, feelings, sensations) and to be guided by their own goals and core values (McCracken and Morley, 2014).

Clients who are struggling with psychological flexibility are likely to be held back by their beliefs about their own abilities to face their feared obstacles. In fact, clients might often believe that they are likely to fail, or that others are judging them for their perceived shortcomings, or believe that they are incapable of managing a potential stressor they are faced with. The following worksheets can be used with clients to help them work toward overcoming their internal obstacles and increasing their psychological flexibility.

Unreliable Psychic

In the *Harry Potter* series, we learn about one of the Hogwarts teachers, Professor Trelawney, who teaches Divination. She often makes terrifying predictions, such as that someone is going to die or that something awful will happen.

Professor Trelawney could serve as an example of an unreliable psychic. Unreliable psychics make many catastrophic predictions, but very few of them actually come true.

Think about it. If there was a psychic in your neighborhood who was known to make ten predictions every day but was only right in her predictions once every 15 years, it would mean that the psychic in this example would make only one correct prediction for every 54,750 incorrect ones![1] Would you trust this psychic?

Our mind is kind of like an unreliable psychic. It might make hundreds or thousands of catastrophizing predictions, most of which don't come true.

Write down or draw a few of your most common catastrophizing thoughts.

---

1   15 years * 365 days * ten predictions/day, not accounting for leap years = 54,750.

Now, pick one of these thoughts (the scariest one) and take a moment to estimate how many times in your life you've had this thought (multiply the approximate number of times you have this thought per day by number of days in a year, and then by the number of years you've been feeling this way).

_____

_____

_____

Now approximate how many times in your life this prediction has come true.

_____

_____

_____

Imagine now that you could talk back to the unreliable psychic, perhaps stating something like, "Thanks for your forewarning, but you and I both know that your predictions tend to not be very reliable." What could you say?

The mind tricksters: Joker and Loki

For some people, especially younger children, the Unreliable Psychic activity might be too challenging. An alternative exercise to teach kids, as well as older clients, about defusion is The Mind Trickster. Tricksters are people or other entities that try to trick us—make us believe something that isn't true. Some examples of well-known tricksters include the Joker, who often tries to trick Batman. The Joker often lies and plays jokes on Batman and other citizens of Gotham City, trying to scare them and confuse them.

Similarly, Loki, Thor's brother, is a trickster god, who often plays jokes on others and spreads lies in order to create confusion and chaos. Finally, brothers Sam and Dean Winchester from the TV show, *Supernatural*, often have to face different kinds of monsters, among them, the Trickster, who frequently uses deception and lies for his personal gain.

The Mind Trickster

(AGES 8–13)

Sometimes our thoughts work kind of like a mind trickster. There are many examples of tricksters—people or other entities who try to trick us and make us believe something that isn't true.

Some examples of well-known tricksters include the Joker from Batman and Loki, Thor's brother. Tricksters might try to confuse us, but we can stand up to them by being a detective like Batman or Sherlock Holmes.

Let's try an example. Write down a scary thought that your own mind trickster might tell you. For example, "If I don't do this perfectly, something bad will happen."

Write out (or say) a thought that scares you sometimes.

_____

_____

Great! Now, let's pretend that you are Batman (or Sherlock Holmes, if you prefer) and you have to figure out if this thought is accurate or if it's your mind trickster trying to confuse you.

To do that, let us look at the evidence for and against this thought. Evidence is a hard fact that you can prove in court.

What is the evidence for this thought? Has this happened before?

_____

_____

What is the evidence against this thought?

_____

_____

What can we say to our mind trickster? For example, "I see you, Trickster/Joker/ Loki. I know what you're trying to do. I know that these are just scary thoughts, they are not accurate and you are just trying to trick me. This is just a thought and I don't have to believe it."

_____

_____

Now, draw a picture of you as Batman (or Sherlock Holmes) arresting the trickster. The trickster might run away and you can catch him again because you are the true superhero. You are the true detective.

In addition to thoughts, many people report that their biggest obstacles include emotions, such as anxiety, depression, and grief, as well as physical sensations, such as chronic pain, chest tightness, or dizziness (especially common in people with anxiety). Unfortunately, most people are so preoccupied with *getting rid of* these emotions and sensations that they are unwilling to partake in meaningful life activities. Most believe that they are unable to live *until* the unwanted sensations and emotions are gone.

According to the ACT model, it is not the uncomfortable sensations that are the problem. Rather, the problem lies in the unwillingness to experience the sensations when they are there (Hayes, 2019). However, getting rid of these sensations might be an unworkable solution. Much like The Pink Unicorn activity we explored in Chapter 2, attempting to force our uncomfortable emotions or sensations to go away can actually intensify them.

For example, one of my clients, let's call her Elizabeth, was fat shamed her entire life by several members of her family and a few of her ex-partners. Elizabeth often reported that she felt as if she were "in a different class" than people who were thinner than her. She avoided taking pictures, going to the beach, dancing, and any other activity that she wanted to do for fear of being made fun of her weight. She believed that she could not enjoy those activities *until* she lost weight. Elizabeth viewed her weight as an obstacle, one she struggled with all her life. In fact, the more she tried to avoid thinking about her weight, untag herself from pictures, and avoid social functions, the more internalized shame she felt about herself and the less authentic she was to herself and to her core values. Instead, her life was focused on avoiding being seen.

In our therapy together, Elizabeth and I worked on changing her relationship with her weight. Rather than seeing it as an obstacle, something that she thought prevented her from going dancing or being in pictures or videos, Elizabeth started seeing her weight as a neutral part of her, the same as her earrings, her hands, and her hair. We worked on her attending functions that she was interested in, such as dancing, as a way of her doing something that was meaningful to her and was true to her core values.

Elizabeth is now a teacher who stands in front of her students every day. She teaches using in-person and video modalities, and although there are still times that she feels self-conscious, her old beliefs and feelings about her weight no longer hold her back from living the kind of life that she wants to live.

The unwillingness to experience painful emotions (such as those related to trauma, depression, anxiety, self-image, or other difficult internal experiences) serves as the biggest predictor of symptom severity (Thompson and Waltz, 2010). On the other hand, mindful awareness of these experiences can actually help the individual be better equipped to face these challenges. In fact, it has been suggested that the non-judgmental mindfulness attitude toward one's symptoms might not only serve to ease their mental health (e.g., PTSD) symptoms but might even create a prophylactic effect in possibly preventing individuals from developing the mental health disorder after being exposed to some of its symptoms (Thompson and Waltz, 2010).

Here are a few activities to support the client in understanding this point. The first of these is The Depression Tormentor, which is a variation on The Pink Unicorn exercise in Chapter 2. The second deals with anxiety and other intrusive and judgmental thoughts.

The Depression Tormentor for Teens/Adults

In the *Harry Potter* series, we learn about terrible monsters—Dementors, whose mere presence makes people feel like things will never be okay again. In a lot of ways that's exactly what depression feel like—cold, numb, and hopeless. Sometimes we might feel sad, sadder than we have ever felt before. At other times, we might feel numb, the kind of numb that is both painless and also excruciating.

Of course, no one *wants* to feel this way. Yet sometimes we do. Sometimes we might feel depressed because of a particular event, such as a breakup, or another painful loss. However, sometimes depression comes "out of nowhere" and sometimes we just feel depressed without any obvious explanation.

When we feel this way, we might naturally try to avoid or run away from this feeling, trying to force ourselves to ignore it, or to pretend like the Dementor isn't there. We might try to distract ourselves, but sooner or later this monster returns.

Take a few moments to imagine this emotion tormentor. Imagine that you are actually looking at this Dementor right in front of you. If you don't know what it looks like, imagine any dark, soul-sucking monster that you might associate with feeling depressed. Now, close your eyes and for a moment, imagine it. Can you visualize it?

Now, keeping your eyes closed, I'm going to ask you to completely erase that monster from your mind and memory for the next 30 seconds. So, do not picture the Dementor, do not even think of the word "Dementor" or "Tormentor" at all.

Ready? Go.

After 30 seconds, please open your eyes.

What was this experience like?

_____

_____

_____

Now, close your eyes again and this time, please focus *only* on this monster in your mind. Think only of the monster. Do not take your mind off of it for the next 30 seconds, don't think of anything else, do *not* get distracted.

Ready? Go.

After 30 seconds, please open your eyes.

What was this experience like?

_____

_____

_____

Alternative exercise

The alternative version of The Depression Tormentor exercise for younger children and for people with learning or developmental disabilities follows. Instead of the client writing in their answers, they can either speak or draw them.

The Depression Tormentor for Kids

In the *Harry Potter* series, we learn about terrible monsters—Dementors, who just by being there make people feel like things will never be okay again. In a lot of ways, that's exactly what many of our emotions feels like—as if things are never going to be okay, leaving us feeling sad, scared, or helpless.

Of course, no one *wants* to feel this way. But sometimes we just do. It's not something we choose, it's just something that happens to us. Sometimes we might feel sad, sometimes we might feel scared, sometimes we might feel angry, and sometimes we might feel numb—we might feel no emotion at all.

Of course, sometimes we might try to run away from these uncomfortable feelings. We might try to distract ourselves, but sooner or later, this monster returns.

Take a few moments to imagine what your monster looks like. Imagine that you are actually looking at this monster right in front of you. Describe it or draw it in the box below.

Now, take a book or a piece of paper and cover up the monster.

You might not be able to see the monster, but it is still there.

Let's do a little exercise to see how it works. Close your eyes and do NOT think of this monster. Do NOT feel afraid. Relax and completely forget that you have ever seen, drawn, or talked about this monster for the next 30 seconds.

Ready? Go.

After 30 seconds, please open your eyes.

What was this experience like?

You might have noticed that we can pretend for a little bit that this monster doesn't exist, but we can't erase it from our minds. So, what if we tried something else?

Take a look at the monster now and draw something to make the monster less scary, to make your monster look friendly, or even funny.

Maybe we can add a few little bows in the monster's hair to make it less scary, or maybe the monster might have a puppy dog that it cares for, or perhaps it wears a silly outfit, like a banana suit, for example. See if you can redraw your monster in this way.

Do You Speak Monster?

Do you ever have thoughts like, "I am not good enough," or "I'm not attractive enough," "I'm not fit enough," or "If people knew the real me, they wouldn't like me very much"? Most people have thoughts like these. They are hurtful or frightening and feel like they are 100 percent real.

Our nervous system fails to see the distinction between the *actual* threat, such as being mauled by a tiger, and a thought in which we *imagine* being eaten by a tiger. In essence, we sometimes become so *fused* with our thoughts, that we react to them emotionally in the same way as if they were actually occurring in this very moment.

Imagine that you are watching one of the *Batman* films and during one of the scenes in which Batman fights the Joker, you might find your own heart pounding and you might even sweat a little. You know that you are not in actual danger, you are not the one fighting the Joker, but your nervous system responds to the movie as if you're a part of it.

In order to reduce the impact that our thoughts might have, we can practice a technique called *defusion*—a way to create some distance between us and the thoughts themselves. For example, when feeling overwhelmed by a scene in a scary zombie film, we can remind ourselves, "This is just another zombie movie, this is not actually happening."

Similarly, we can practice creating some distance between us and our thoughts. For example, when having a thought such as, "If I don't exercise, I will be unattractive and no one will love me," we can instead remind ourselves, "This is just another self-image movie. I am having a thought that if I don't exercise, I will be unattractive and no one will love me."

We can think of our thoughts as our own internal movie themes, often related to the fears of losing or never obtaining our greatest passions and desires. Some of these themes include social belonging/connection, personal growth and achievement/ability, and self-image.

See if you can identify some of the common "movie themes" that might play out in your mind.

Movie themes:
Social belonging and connection:

- I will make a mistake, it will be humiliating, and everyone will laugh at me and then reject and abandon me.
- I will lose someone I care about (to death, abandonment, or rejection).
- If I try to get close to someone, I will be rejected.
- If people really get to know me, they will reject or abandon me.

Personal growth, achievement, and ability:

- If I try this and fail, I will lose something I care about (job, opportunity, status, etc.).
- If I try something/take a chance/try to change, I will fail.

Personal danger:

- If I trust someone, they will hurt me.
- If I am not in control over this situation, I will not be safe.
- Because I've been hurt before, it means that it is highly likely to happen again.

Self-image:

- This part of me is unacceptable and no one can love or accept me until I change this part of myself.
- Until I can change this part of myself, I am not allowed to be happy or to do things that make me happy.

Now practice rewriting some of your common thoughts as a defusion exercise. Think of it as translating from Monster language into your own language. For example, "My social belonging story is telling me that if I try to get close to someone, I will be rejected." Alternatively, you can say, "My thought is telling me that if I try to get close to someone, I will be rejected" or "I'm having that same old thought/movie playing out in my mind that if I try to get close to someone, I will be rejected."

See if you can try this out in the space below.

_____

_____

_____

_____

_____

_____

_____

_____

_____

Making emotion monsters less threatening

For people with severe anxiety, especially social anxiety, the above defusion activity might be very challenging. Similarly, it might be too difficult for younger children. The following is an alternative activity designed specifically for individuals with anxiety disorders. The goal here is to foster defusion practice through making the thoughts seem silly and ridiculous.

Please note: although this exercise can be helpful for individuals with anxiety, it is *not* recommended for individuals who survived violent trauma, such as abuse or assault.

Monster Made Ridiculous

(ALL AGES)

Sometimes our anxiety can cause our imagination to think of the scariest scenarios, most of which will never come true. Very often, we assume that the scary thought will happen exactly as we imagine it and we assume that it is accurate.

The truth is that we have many scary thoughts throughout the day and many of them are no truer than a silly thought, such as "I am a banana." However, our anxiety makes us *feel* like these scary thoughts are likely to come true.

One way that we can face this anxiety monster is similar to how Harry Potter and his friends faced a Boggart—a shape-shifting monster who turns into whatever scares us the most. The best way to face this kind of fear-inducing anxiety monster is to make it seem ridiculous. For example, it might be a lot less scary if this monster was wearing a banana suit or another silly outfit while trying to yell its scary messages at you through a megaphone.

Draw your anxiety monster below but make it look ridiculous. If you can, please feel free to add some things that it might say to you as a speech bubble in a comic book.

Humour alone can help alleviate anxiety. However, humour with reframing can help participants to reduce their anxiety about a stressful situation (e.g., test-taking) even more (Ford *et al.*, 2017). The Ridiculous activity includes both: humour and reframing of anxiety as a silly-looking monster.

Another example of this activity is the Can You Make It Worse? exercise, which is primarily designed for individuals with social anxiety but can be utilized for other types of anxiety on a case-by-case basis. Most individuals with social anxiety (and other forms of anxiety) might imagine their worst-case scenario (e.g., "What if I make a mistake during my presentation?") but rarely think of what will happen next. This exercise is designed to allow the individual to defuse from their thought, as well as to reframe this idea in a humorous manner.

I was working with a client with social anxiety; let's call her "Wendy." Wendy was very passionate about skateboarding but was terrified about falling off her skateboard in front of others. When I asked her what would happen if she did, she stated that she would feel "very embarrassed" and that some people might laugh at her and think, "Wow, that girl doesn't know how to skate."

I then asked her, "Can you make it worse?"

At first, Wendy was confused. She was trying too hard to not be silly and to not feel embarrassed, so when I asked her to imagine the situation being even more embarrassing, she initially wasn't sure how to proceed. However, after a few moments, she identified several factors that would make it worse:

- if people laughed out loud
- if people pointed fingers
- if people recorded it and put it on social media.

I then asked her again, "Can you make it worse?"

Wendy thought about it and said, "If the video went viral, that would be worse."

I asked her again, "Can you make it worse?"

She thought about it and then laughed, "If the news showed up and made a news segment about it."

After a few more tries, Wendy identified several other situations that would make her falling off her skateboard a more embarrassing experience and then we put it all together and then read it as an imaginal exposure exercise, where the individual imagines their worst case scenario coming true. Here is what Wendy said:

"I am very nervous but I decide to try skateboarding at my school. I try to balance but I fall down. A few hundred students are coming out of their classes and they are all laughing at me and recording me. Teachers cancel classes, so that everyone can come outside and see me falling. The news vans and helicopters show up and it is the number one recurring segment of the day.

The video of me falling is also trending on all social media platforms and then is played over and over on the marquis in Times Square in New York. The paparazzi stalk me to take pictures of 'the girl who fell' and everyone in the world knows that it's me."

Wendy was later able to practice purposely falling off her skateboard in her school and reported that it went "well" and that no one laughed at her but that she was able to giggle at her own experience, remembering the Can You Make It Worse? activity.

Can You Make It Worse?

Very often we might feel overwhelmed and anxious, especially in social situations. Sometimes we might fear making a social mistake, such as falling down while trying to learn to skate or making a mistake during our presentation.

We often only think of the worst-case scenario but don't usually think *past that*. In this exercise, we are going to try to think of your worst-case scenario but we are going to try to make it worse, and even more "over the top" and ridiculous than you could ever possibly imagine.

To do this, let's first identify one example of something you're nervous about, such as making a mistake in public and people judging you or laughing at you. Write out your feared outcome below.

_____

_____

_____

_____

Now, see if you can make it worse. This might sound silly (and it's meant to). Let's see if we can imagine the situation unfolding in an even more extreme and ridiculous way, such as your mistake becoming the #1 trending story on Twitter or the front page of the *New York Times*.

_____

_____

_____

_____

Can you make it worse? Are there any ways that you can make this story even more ridiculous and "over the top"?

_____

_____

_____

_____

Now, see if you can put your entire story together from start to finish, such as the experience of you falling down (for example) and your story making worldwide news.

_____

_____

_____

_____

_____

_____

_____

_____

_____

Now that we've looked at the "over the top" scenario, what do you think would be the most likely scenario if your feared situation came true?

_____

_____

_____

_____

_____

_____

_____

_____

_____

_____

_____

The should monster

Arguably one of the biggest obstacles that many people face has to do with *should-related* thoughts. These cognitive distortions (or cognitive fusions, if you are an ACT practitioner) can cause the individual to be so restricted in their thinking that they might not realize that they have more choices and possibilities than they think in most situations.

The next activity is a coloring exercise intended for people of all ages. I used to think that coloring exercises were only for children. I realized later that it was my own rigid "should" programming that made me restricted in how I saw the world. In the past few years, I've not only begun to implement coloring exercises with my adult clients, I've started using them myself as a way to practice being mindful and present, and also as a way to get in touch with my creativity. I would like to invite you to not only use the exercise below with your clients but also to try it out yourself.

Coloring Outside of the Box

We have many thoughts that contain the word "should." Some of these thoughts reflect our morals, such as "we shouldn't lie" or "I shouldn't hurt other people." These are great morals to have.

However, the word "should" also sometimes shows up in certain rules that we might have created or other people might have taught us, such as "I should never make a mistake" or "I should never color outside of the lines."

Although these rules can be helpful as general guidelines, if we follow them too stringently, we might miss our opportunity to learn. For example, some mistakes can even lead to new scientific discoveries. Sometimes if we take the wrong route, we might discover a new one.

Let's try this. Color the following shapes by staying inside the lines. Please try to use a different color or shading for each separate shape.

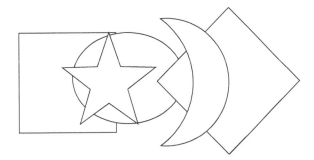

Great job!

Next try to color the same shapes but now give yourself the permission to color outside of the lines or to create new shapes altogether. Suspend all coloring rules for this exercise and try something you've never tried before.

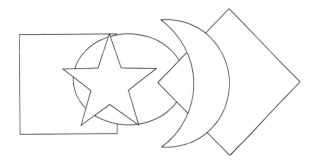

What did you notice the first time you tried this exercise? And the second time? How were they different?

_____

_____

Your clients will likely have faced many setbacks and heartbreaks before they have ever met you. There will be times when you will feel excited and encouraged to help them. And there will also be times when you might doubt whether you are being helpful. Your own monsters might be showing up too and I have found that the inverse of our greatest fears is the foundation of our greatest strength. The very notion that you might worry about whether you are helpful to your clients already shows how much you care. You wouldn't be in this job if you didn't.

Know this: your mere presence with your clients, your willingness to be present not only with their monsters but also with your own, already shows a greater amount of courage and heroism than you might have ever known was possible. And just as your client is learning to partake in their own hero's journey, you are already embarking on yours. Your every action makes a difference. From the bottom of my heart, thank you for saving lives on a regular basis. You might not always know this, but you are incredible. Thank you for being wonderful.

Chapter 4

FINDING A SUPERHERO MENTOR

He came into my office 25 minutes late. Sweat was dripping from his face. His arms were shaking, holding onto two walking sticks.

Let's call him "Chuck."

He grunted as he walked, his face grimacing from the pain. I got up to move the chair closer to him, so that he could sit down.

"Don't," he said.

His breathing heavy, his face somehow looking at least 20 years older than his age, Chuck finally made it to his chair. But he made it on his own.

Chuck told me about his injuries. He was hurt during his deployment and was supposed to be in a wheelchair. However, Chuck refused the wheelchair and insisted on using the walking sticks instead. He was also issued a disabled person parking placard for his car, which he also refused to use.

Chuck was on limited duty and was facing a medical separation from the military. He believed himself to be "weak" and "broken." He said that he didn't feel like he could be the kind of superhero dad to his toddler son that he wanted to be because he couldn't run around with him. "I can't even help my wife carry the groceries, you know?" He added, "She carries them all herself now, even the heavy ones."

Chuck shamed himself for developing a disability and PTSD. He isolated from his friends and family and spent most of his time alone, believing himself to be "a failure."

I asked Chuck if he knew anything about

Batgirl, a superhero from DC Comics. Chuck stated that he knew a lot about Batman but not a lot about Batgirl. We then proceeded to talk about Batgirl's origin story. Batgirl (real name: Barbara Gordon) was a librarian by day and a superhero by night. Then, one tragic day, she was shot (and possibly assaulted) by an evil villain, the Joker, paralyzing her from the waist down.

Barbara Gordon then goes to therapy to work on her PTSD. Over time, she realizes that she might not need her legs to be a superhero. She realizes that she is still a librarian and that she can use her library skills to become a new kind of superhero—Oracle. She uses technology to help other superheroes and operates a worldwide communications network.

As Chuck and I talked about Barbara Gordon's journey of becoming Oracle, he smiled. He actually looked up at me, which was in contrast to his usual position of looking down in shame. We talked about how a change in someone's ability does not have to change their superhero status.

The next session was the first time Chuck had showed up on time to his session. He rolled in on his wheelchair, grinning at me. "You won't believe how fast I am in this thing, Doc!"

Chuck shared with me that he was able to chase his son around the backyard and was able to help his wife with groceries in the past week. It was the first time that he seemed to realize that much like in Barbara Gordon's case, his heroic self never changed. And this realization empowered him.

Like Chuck, many people believe themselves to be "weak," "broken," or somehow "defective" when they are going through the most challenging time of their life. They often fail to realize that their experiences strengthen them, and that facing their adversity is not a sign of weakness but rather the foundation of their greatest strength.

As outside observers, you might notice other people's experiences with adversity and be in awe of their courage and perseverance. Yet, when you are the one struggling, you might forget to see how many mountains you've already climbed. You might forget how much you've already overcome and might not realize that to an outsider, you already look like a superhero.

Sometimes when we forget to find the strength in our experiences, we can find it in our heroes. Fictional heroes (as well as real-life role models) can serve as a powerful reminder of what we are capable of. In fact, when people identify with a hero and that hero has high self-efficacy (e.g., manages adversity), it can affect their own sense of self-efficacy (Isberner *et al.*, 2019).

Like Chuck, any of us might also benefit from a heroic role model, who can remind us that we are not alone in our experiences or struggles, who can remind us that sometimes the worst experiences we have ever had might become our most powerful teachers. Don't get me wrong, pain and suffering are not gifts. And yet, sometimes they unlock our inner superpowers that we did not even know existed. In order to help our clients to unlock their deepest strengths, sometimes it can be helpful to assist them in first finding a heroic mentor who can guide them through this process.

What Is a Personal Hero?

Personal heroes can help people to understand what they are going through and inspire people to stand up for themselves or others. A personal hero is someone who can inspire us, someone who can remind us of what we stand for.

A personal hero can be anyone—it can be someone we know very well or someone we don't know at all. For example, a personal hero can be a family member, such as a parent or a grandparent, whether they are living or no longer alive. Similarly, a personal hero could be a teacher or a coach, or someone else that you might look up to.

A personal hero could also be someone you have never met, someone like a professional athlete, a movie or a TV star, a singer, a YouTube influencer, or a writer. For some of us, our personal heroes might also include fictional characters that inspire us, like Batman, Wonder Woman, or Dumbledore. See if you can take a few moments to think about who some of your heroes might be. You can pick one, two, or several heroes. Write their names or draw them below.

Now take a few moments to think about what you like about your favorite hero(es). For example, you might admire them for being courageous even when they are scared, for helping others, for being kind and compassionate, for being funny, or for standing up for what they believe in. Please write out or draw what you admire about your favorite heroes.

Can you think of a time when you felt sad, scared, or alone? What was going on then? Please write out or draw your answer below.

☆

If any of your heroes could be there for you during that time, which would you wish to have been there for you? What do you imagine they would have said to you? How would they try to support or encourage you? Please write out or draw your answer below.

Positive role models can help people to be inspired to take action, to face their fears, and to share their experiences with others (Hoffman *et al.*, 2019; Isberner *et al.*, 2019; Scarlet, 2020). Recently, I was working with a teen client, who struggled with depression, social anxiety disorder, and panic attacks. Let's call her "Kelly." Kelly experienced public shaming by her elementary school teacher, and bullying by her classmates while in middle school. Over the years, Kelly's anxiety and depression continued to worsen. She frequently avoided class presentations and asking questions in class. Over time, her panic attacks became so severe that Kelly was unable to attend school, spending nearly 6 months at home. She was able to do all her schoolwork but was unable to interact with other students or communicate about what she was going through.

When Kelly and I met, she disclosed that she was a fan of the TV show, *Supernatural*. Briefly, *Supernatural* is an American television show about two brothers, Sam and Dean Winchester, who hunt supernatural monsters, such as demons, werewolves, and vampires, saving people and preventing numerous disasters and atrocities. Kelly mentioned that she strongly identified with the older brother, Dean Winchester, whose character often kept his feelings to himself, but felt responsible for other people's wellbeing. Kelly mentioned that she often felt uncomfortable sharing her feelings with others but wanted to be able to help others to face their own struggles. Kelly completed the Origin Story activity and identified her personal hero as Dean Winchester. When asked what Dean would say to her if she could ask him for guidance, Kelly replied, "Dean would remind me that I've already been facing many of these monsters for years. He would remind me to be a hunter—

to help people in any way I can and to face my monsters instead of running away from them."

In identifying with Dean in this way, Kelly was able to create a list of actions she was willing to take in order to train to become a version of a monster hunter in real life. Specifically, Kelly practiced going to the mall with me and with her parents. She practiced eating by herself, asking for help, doing silly and embarrassing things on purpose (e.g., asking for directions to a movie theater while standing in front of it), and finally was able to return to her school. Kelly then worked on supporting her classmates who were going through mental health challenges and planned to start a mental health club in her school (unfortunately, the Covid-19 pandemic prevented her from being able to complete this last task). Kelly was able to complete therapy by frequently asking herself, "What would Dean do in this situation?" By identifying her role model and following his guidance (which technically was her own voice of wisdom), Kelly was able to better manage her anxiety and depression, and become her own version of a hero in real life.

In Kelly's case, she was already coming into therapy to receive treatment for anxiety and depression. However, some clients, especially younger children, or even adults who have not had a lot of experience in talking about their mental health, might struggle to even realize that they need help. It is for this reason that in 1985 Marvel Comics and the National Committee for Prevention of Child Abuse (NCPCA) partnered up to release a special issue of the *Spider-Man* comic book, in which Spider-Man discovers that a little boy is being sexually abused by his babysitter. Spider-Man then shares his own story of being sexually abused by a young man, helping the young boy to understand that even superheroes might experience abuse and that it is okay to ask for help. That boy is then able to report the incident to his parents with Spider-Man's help.

In a subsequent research study, 73 children from second to sixth grade (ages 7–11) were shown the comic. One of the boys reported that the comics depicted exactly what he experienced in terms of being molested by a teenage neighbor. The boy reported that having had the comic earlier would have helped him understand that he had the right to tell his mother about the abuse and reported that reading the comic gave him the courage to do so (Garbarino, 1987).

Superheroes and other fictional characters and stories have been shown to help readers to obtain a sense of "dual empathy"— simultaneously processing their own thoughts, feelings, and experiences, as well as those of the fictional characters (Dill-Shackleford, Vinney, and Hopper-Losenicky, 2016). In fact, research studies related to reading science fiction or fantasy books such as *Harry Potter* demonstrate that people who read these works are more likely to be empathic toward typically stigmatized groups (e.g., homeless individuals, immigrants, LGBTQ individuals) and show lower levels of prejudice against them (Vezzali *et al.*, 2015). Furthermore, research related to reading fantasy and science fiction also shows that in connection with these heroes and stories, readers are more likely to be able to better manage arguments with their romantic partners (Stern *et al.*, 2019) and be potentially more interested in engaging with science (Menadue and Jacups, 2018).

Studies have revealed additional benefits of heroic role models when priming participants to think about their favorite superhero, or to embody them, include increasing self-esteem, and increasing altruistic and health-related behaviors in children and adults (Cuddy, Wilmuth, and Carney, 2012; Peña and Chen, 2017; Rosenberg, Baughman, and Bailenson, 2013). For example, in their 2012 study, researchers at Cornell University (Wansink, Shimizu, and Camps, 2012) asked a group of children to pick between apple slices and French fries. Not surprisingly, only 9 percent of children chose apples, which means that 91 percent of children chose French fries as their food of choice. The children were then primed with one question, "What do you think Batman would eat?" Most of the children stated that Batman would pick apples over French fries. Following this superhero priming question, the children were 50 percent more likely to choose apples over French fries (Wansink *et al.*, 2012). These results suggest that people might be able to at least temporarily change their behavior when inspired to do so by a hero they admire. A similar finding by White and Carlson (2015) suggests that dressing up like their favorite characters can help children to maintain attention on task, such as homework. This means that if our clients identify with particular heroes, embodying those heroes can positively influence a change in that person's behavior.

Here are two activities that you can practice with your clients in terms of embodying their favorite hero. The first (Acting Like a Superhero) is for kids and adults of just about any age. The second (Engaging in Daily Activities Like a Superhero) is intended for older teens and adults.

Acting Like a Superhero

Very often when we are going through a tough time, we might not want to talk to anyone, we might sit or lie down, maybe curl into a ball, and take a posture that makes us look smaller. However, we know that standing up for 2 minutes with our arms at our sides like Superman or Wonder Woman can make us feel more self-confident over time.[1]

Let's try this out now. If you are able to stand up, let's stand. Otherwise, you can do this posture while sitting down. Please place your arms at your sides and imagine yourself in a superhero costume, like Superman or Wonder Woman would wear. Try this out for 2 minutes.

How did that feel?

Try taking this Superhero posture before you start doing a task you don't want to do, such as your homework or exercise. Is there a special outfit or accessory you'd like to wear to fully embody your superhero self? Maybe you'd like to wear a cape, a tiara, a Harry Potter necklace, or a Green Lantern ring?

Please draw yourself standing (or sitting) in your superhero posture and write down or draw any clothes or accessories you'd like to be wearing to help you complete your homework, exercise, or other tasks.

---

1   Cuddy *et al.* (2012).

☆

Engaging in Daily Activities Like a Superhero

by Lanaya Ethington
(Used with permission)

Bring to mind an action that you do every day. It could be something like brushing your teeth, washing your face, making breakfast, or taking a shower. For this exercise, you may want to choose an action that you can do while you are sitting down. Or you may choose to stand up and do an action if you are able.

Get into a comfortable position that commands dignity and respect. I typically have my feet on the floor, my hands in my lap, my eyes gently closed, feeling my shoulders fall away from my ears.

Bring awareness to the breath.

To begin, I invite you to bring your present self to your daily activity. Your present self is just whatever is here right now. Whatever thoughts, emotions, physical sensations you may be experiencing. If you feel comfortable, I invite you to go through the physical motions of a daily activity, from start to finish. So if you are brushing your teeth, for example, go through the motions of opening the drawer with the toothpaste, uncapping the toothpaste, putting it on your toothbrush, raising the toothbrush to your mouth, and so on. There is no rush to this activity, and your pace during it may be different than your pace during the day. When you reach the end of the daily activity, start again from the beginning, and keep doing so for the next minute or so.

Now, you can stop your activity, no matter where you are in the process, and come back to your present-moment stance. Now, I invite you to step into your "superhero self," whatever that means to you. It may be a version of yourself that has superhero qualities, it may be the embodiment of a specific character, it may be the augmentation of a characteristic you really admire. It could be superhero endurance, unending amounts of patience, or the ability to get up if you've been knocked down. As you embody your "superhero self," I invite you to notice any change in your posture, any change in your facial expression, any change to your thoughts or emotions, any changes to your physical sensations.

I invite you now to begin again the physical movements of your daily activity, using the stance of your superhero self. Notice the difference of how it feels to move, in your body, using your superhero self. Notice the thoughts you experience, as you go about your daily activity from this stance. Notice the emotions that are present, as you engage in your activity.

You may slow your activity, and let your hands drop, and return to the here and now. Let's turn our attention back to the breath.

Villains and antiheroes

Inevitably, when I teach the course on Superhero Therapy and we talk about heroic role models, someone asks, "But what do I do if my client identifies with a *villain*?" This is a wonderful question to ask and one that deserves a lot of attention, as this is an important topic to talk about. In fact, many people are quite fond of villains and antiheroes. Does this mean that we, as clinicians, need to assess our clients for homicidal ideation? My answer: not any more or less than we would otherwise when working with those particular clients. The mere identification with a villainous character does not indicate that the client has homicidal tendencies. I tend to favor villainous characters or antiheroes, as they can often be more interesting than some of the heroes that we see or read about.

The most important question we can ask a client who likes a villain (or any character, for that matter) is "What do you like about that character?" Many clients might see a representation of what they might be missing in their own lives, such as the freedom to enjoy themselves, or standing up for what they believe in, justice, or the ability to display anger. Or perhaps they identify with the villain's (or antihero's) origin story, which often includes abuse, neglect, bullying, or rejection. Some people see themselves in that character's story and therefore might feel a sense of compassion toward them. Others might vicariously live out their desires or fantasies through the villainous character. For example, some villains (and antiheroes) might believe that they are justified in killing bad people who have wronged them. For some viewers who are holding onto a lot of pain and anger from a past injustice, seeing bad people being brought to justice might be cathartic. Inquiring about this can help to guide the course of the client's treatment to help them better address their unresolved hurt and anger.

Similarly, some individuals might be intrigued by the villain's lifestyle. For example, some villains are able to be open with their sexuality, most have their own schedules, and most don't have to answer to anyone. For many watching or reading about these characters, they might see a representation of a wish fulfilment, such as freedom. Think about most adults' (and kids') daily schedules: get up, do work, have dinner, go to sleep, repeat. Many people do not have enough time in their day, week, or month to do what they would like to do—to have fun. But villains get to live by their own calendars. They can have ice cream for breakfast. They can go to the beach in the middle of the day. In short, villains get to have fun and they get to express themselves. What would it look like if our clients learned these messages from the villainous characters that they like, but in a productive way?

A few years ago, I was working with a young woman; let's call her "Jane." Jane came in for support with obsessive-compulsive disorder (OCD) and social anxiety disorder. She also reported that she was the only woman in her workplace and the only person who had not been given a raise in 5 years.

In her first session with me, Jane self-described as "mousy." She said that it was hard for her to speak up for herself and to be assertive. When asked about her favorite fandoms, she mentioned that she loved *Star Wars*. In particular, Jane said that she loved Kylo Ren (the main antagonist in the third trilogy). When Jane mentioned his name, she sat up, propped up her body, and projected her voice. In other words, when Jane mentioned the name of her favorite character, she was no longer that "mousy" woman who walked through my door. She was Jane—a powerful woman. When I asked her what she liked about this character, Jane mentioned that she liked that "he gets angry and is not afraid to show it."

Although Jane was not initially aware of this, she was holding onto a lot of anger and resentment toward her boss and many of the workers in her company. Over the upcoming months, we worked on her channeling her dark side (but without killing people), where she embodied the posture of someone connected with the dark side. She also practiced expressing her anger through assertive communication role-plays in the session. After a few months, she was able to ask her boss to meet with her and requested a raise.

And she got it!

To celebrate, Jane and her husband went to Disneyland, where she built her own lightsaber. Jane continues to practice her "dark side" assertiveness skills and now enjoys cosplaying as various villainous characters. Her connection to these characters allowed her to practice her own self-expression skills, which helped her to reduce her social anxiety and OCD.

Sidekicks

In helping clients to find their own strengths from their favorite heroes (or villains), the most important stance we, as mental health providers, can take in Superhero Therapy is one of non-judgmental curiosity and unconditional positive regard. In helping the client to become the hero of their journey, our job is to be their sidekick and their biggest fan.

Some clients might have never previously felt supported by others while other clients might believe that they ought to be able to handle any obstacles they are facing on their own. However, every hero, even a superhero, has sidekicks. Sidekicks are essentially the client's sources of support, which can be present in person, virtually, or even in a fictional sense.

The following activity is one way you can help your client to identify their potential sidekicks.

Identifying Your Sidekicks

Every hero has a sidekick or a support system. For example, Batman has Robin, Superman has the Justice League, and Harry Potter has Ron and Hermione.

Sidekicks are any people (or animals) who can support you in life. These can be your family members, your friends, your pets, your neighbors, people with whom you play online, members of your favorite fandom, or maybe even fictional characters.

First, what are some of the qualities that sidekicks have?

They are reliable, supportive, and kind. They will be there when you need them. They believe in you.

Is there anyone you can think of in your life, either a real-life person, a pet, or even a fictional character, that has ever been there for you when you needed them, at least once in your life? Write out their names or draw their pictures below.

Sidekick identification can help your clients to realize that they are not alone and that they have at least some forms of support from others, at least some of the time. In the event that the client is unable to identify any sidekicks, this activity can be extended to consider the kinds of sidekicks the client would like to have and how they might go about receiving this kind of support.

For many of your clients, their number one source of support is you. They might never tell you but it's true. As mentioned in an earlier chapter, they are likely having imagined conversations with you in their mind during their most challenging times, often not realizing that they are essentially completing the hero activity with you being their mentor. In turn, think about what your client might be going through during the times in between your sessions. Think of what you would want to say to them before they leave your session. Think about what kind of message would you like them to hold onto during their most challenging times because your words matter. Your actions matter. Because you truly make a difference.

Chapter 5

MINDFULNESS SPELL

Chances are that you have probably heard of mindfulness and have utilized it with your clients. Mindfulness has become one of the most utilized skills for therapists and for good reason. In fact, regular mindfulness practice can reduce anxiety and depression (Roemer *et al.*, 2009), reduce symptoms of PTSD (Bormann, Hurst, and Kelly, 2013), improve mood (Epel *et al.*, 2009), improve brain functioning (Davidson *et al.*, 2003), and potentially prolong lifespan (Carlson *et al.*, 2015; Epel and Lithgow, 2014).

Many people believe that they are "not good at mindfulness" because they are unable to "shut off their mind." However, mindfulness practices are not meant to literally stop our thoughts. In fact, our brains are not designed to "shut off and not think." Instead, mindfulness practices are meant to help people tune into their thoughts, feelings, and sensations without judging these experiences. The key is to notice when our attention drifts from the current task and to gently bring the attention back to the task at hand without judgment (Epel *et al.*, 2009). Interestingly, when people are mindful of an unpleasant emotion, such as grief or anxiety, or when they are mindfully engaging in an unpleasant task, such as washing the dishes, they tend to report feeling happier than when they are purposely trying to distract from this unpleasant activity or emotion (Killingsworth and Gilbert, 2010).

When people are engaged in a mindful activity, one that either requires or naturally has their attention, they are more likely to exhibit mindfulness-like patterns in their physiological and neurological patterns of activity. However, when people are resting, bored, or engaging in a mindless task, their brain is likely to turn toward its natural default mode. In fact, researchers have recently identified a default mode network (DMN), which consists of specific areas of the brain (i.e., dorsal and medial prefrontal cortices, medial and lateral parietal cortices, and specific regions of the medial and lateral temporal cortices; Sheline *et al.*, 2009). The default mode network is engaged in assuring our survival, and as such, it is usually scanning for possible danger, including social rejection, ruminating about past events, or risk assessing the future. The DMN is said to be more active in people with clinical depression and it seems that increasing mindfulness practices can reduce the activity in the DMN and possibly reduce depression (Sheline *et al.*, 2009).

On the one hand, it makes sense for humans to think about our past and to plan for our future. After all, learning from our past and being able to be prepared for the future is essential for our survival. However, it does also seem that practicing mindfulness can be extremely beneficial for our clients' mental and physical health (Epel *et al.*, 2009; Roemer *et al.*, 2009). Yet, one of the biggest obstacles to clients practicing mindfulness appears to be the fear that if they allow themselves to feel their unwanted emotions, they might "break." It is true that in some instances, when people first tune into their unprocessed grief, for example, they might sob for an extended period of time. However, they do not cry forever. Eventually, they stop, often feeling both exhausted and relieved. A metaphor I often use with clients is that of a fizzy drink (an extension of the activity from Chapter 2).

Here is an example of a conversation I often have with my clients:

Therapist: Have you ever had a fizzy drink?
Client: Sure. Many times.
T: What happens to fizzy drinks when we shake them for a long time?
C: I guess the pressure builds up?
T: That's right. The pressure builds up. And what happens if it builds up too much?
C: I guess it could explode.
T: Right! The bottle could explode, releasing the pressure. Kind of like our feelings. If we keep them under the lid for too long without releasing the pressure, we might also explode. Has that ever happened to you?
C: Yeah. I once blew up on my brother. We yelled at each other for a while.
T: It makes sense that you blew up on each other. It sounds like there was a lot of pressure built up.
C: Yeah, there was. And see, that's why I'm afraid to show my emotions. If I do, I might blow up again.
T: I can understand that concern. What happened when you blew up on your brother? Did you keep blowing up forever?

C: No. I guess it subsided after a while.
T: Right. Just like a fizzy drink doesn't explode forever, our emotions might erupt if we keep them under a tight lid, but even in that case, they eventually settle. However, ideally, we tune into our emotions to reduce that pressure regularly.
C: How do I do that?
T: Think of it like tuning into your Spidey senses of connecting with the Force.

In order to assist clients with understanding mindfulness, it can be helpful to use experiential exercises, such as a guided meditation practice. The following meditation exercise can be used with clients of nearly all ages (7 and above), and is a guided meditation practice that a therapist can read to the client. Keep in mind that survivors of sexual assault can sometimes be triggered by mindfulness exercises that bring their attention to the sensations of their body. Hence, when working with survivors of sexual assault, this exercise can be done in small segments throughout the course of therapy to teach clients how to use mindfulness to self-regulate when they are experiencing trauma-related triggers. Since many survivors of sexual abuse, especially childhood sexual abuse, tend to struggle with mindfulness, which subsequently contributes to higher PTSD symptoms (Daigneault *et al.*, 2016), it is important to introduce mindfulness as a coping tool for survivors of abuse or assault, though in some instances, it might be useful to do so gradually.

Meditation: Tuning into Your Spidey Senses

This is a guided meditation practice that a therapist can read to the client.

Bring your attention to your breathing. Notice how your body is moving with each inhale and each exhale (a brief pause). Notice the sensations of your body, as a way of tuning into your Spidey senses.

Notice the sensations of your feet as they are making contact with the ground (a brief pause). If the sensation of your feet is not available or possible, please focus on the sensations of your arms, or the sensations of your lips, instead.

Take a moment to notice that at this moment, you are right here, you are not late for anything, and you are not in a rush to get anywhere. You are right here in this moment, doing exactly what you should be doing.

And at any time, if you get distracted or overwhelmed, you can silently ask yourself, "Where are my feet?" (or arms, or lips) to gently bring yourself back to the present moment, as if using your spider web to bring you back down to the ground.

Take a few moments to notice any physical sensations that you might be feeling in this moment, such as pain or tension. Take a few moments to breathe while noticing these Spidey sensations (a brief pause). Not trying to make them go away and not forcing them to be stronger than they are. Just noticing these sensations as information, as a part of your own Spidey senses (a brief pause).

Now, take a few moments to bring your attention to your emotions. Our emotions are kind of like the weather—they are always changing. Sometimes we might feel one way, and sometimes, another way. See if you can take a few moments to simply notice how you are feeling in this moment, as a way of sharpening your Spidey senses—just noticing your emotions at this time (a brief pause).

Now take a few moments to focus on the sounds around you, activating your Spidey senses while allowing yourself to gently breathe as you're doing so (a brief pause).

Now take a few moments to notice the temperature in this room (a brief pause). Take a few moments to notice if there are any smells you can detect in this environment, while continuing to breathe (a brief pause).

Now, take another minute to notice the sensations of your hands and feet in this moment (a brief pause). And then bringing your awareness back to this room, take a few breaths, and take as much time as you need to open your eyes and come back into the room.

What did you notice during this exercise? Feel free to write or draw your answer below.

Learning to observe emotions

Clients with a history of trauma and/or panic attacks often have a difficult time trusting their emotional experiences. Many might feel unsafe to experience these emotions, despite the fact that purposely suppressing these emotions tends to intensify them. Here is an activity I sometimes use with my clients to help them face their uncomfortable internal experiences in a gradual way. It is a guided meditation practice that a therapist can read to the client.

Dog Park for Teens/Adults

(AGES 13 AND UP)

This is a guided meditation practice that a therapist can read to the client.

Sometimes our emotions feel like an enormous monster, chasing us as we are trying to run away to safety. However, there is a trick. Like Pennywise, the scary clown from *IT*, the monster feeds on fear and avoidance, meaning that it becomes scarier and more powerful when we run away from it, but smaller and less intimidating when we face it.

And there is another trick—the monster is more powerful when you face all its parts together. But if you break apart each part of the monster, you can be more powerful when you face it.

Let's look at your symptoms. Many people who are struggling with panic attacks, depression, or trauma-related feelings might experience some of these symptoms. Check or circle the ones that apply to you:

- tightness and tension in the neck and shoulders
- tightness in the chest
- feeling out of breath
- heart pounding
- sweating
- shaking
- feeling lightheaded
- stomach discomfort
- feeling like things are not real
- flushed cheeks
- other _____

Imagine for a few moments that you are taking your dog to a dog park (even if you don't actually have a dog). When the dog is on the leash, it's probably excited, hyper, and can't wait to be let off the leash. But once you take the leash off, the dog can run around freely to let some of its energy out until it feels calm and settled.

We are now going to do a similar exercise with each of the sensations above. We are going to start with the least uncomfortable, the least distressing sensation from the ones you picked above. Got one?

Okay, now imagine that you can zoom in your attention to only focus on this symptom or sensation. For example, if you picked "sweating" then focus your entire attention now on just noticing how sweaty you are feeling in this moment.

Great! Now we are going to imagine that you took this sensation to the dog park and took the leash off. That means that just for a few minutes, we are going to only focus on this sensation while allowing it to be here, allowing it to be as strong or as weak as it needs to be.

If you are willing, I'm going to ask you to close your eyes and focus only on this one sensation and fully allow it to be here, as if allowing it to run around in the dog park.

Ready?

Go!

How did it go? What did you notice? Was it tolerable just to focus on this sensation?

Would you be willing to try another one?

See if you can focus on each of these sensations one at a time for at least 1 to 2 minutes.

What did you notice over time? Write or draw in the box below.

The more we can let our emotions "off the leash," one element at a time, the easier it can be for us to face these emotions over time.

Dog Park for Kids

This is a guided meditation practice that a therapist can read to the client.

Sometimes our emotions feel like an enormous monster, chasing us as we are trying to run away. However, there is a trick. The monster feeds on fear and gets bigger if we avoid it. That means it becomes scarier and more powerful when we run away from it, but smaller and less scary when we face it. And there is another trick—the monster is more powerful when you face all of its parts together. But if you break apart each part of the monster, you can be more powerful when you face it.

Let's look at your feelings and break them up into separate parts. Check or circle the ones that apply to you:

- tightness in the neck and shoulders
- tightness in the chest
- feeling out of breath
- heart beating fast
- sweating
- feeling shaky
- feeling dizzy
- stomach ache
- feeling as if you are in a dream
- hot cheeks
- something else _____

Imagine for a few moments that you are taking a dog to a dog park (even if you don't actually have a dog). When the dog is on the leash, he's probably excited, hyper, and can't wait to be let off the leash. But once you take the leash off, the dog can run around freely to let some of his energy out until he feels calm.

Now, we are going to do a similar exercise with each of the feelings that you feel. Pick one feeling from the ones that you circled above, such as feeling shaky, or feeling out of breath. Got one?

Okay, now imagine that you can zoom in your attention to only focus on this feeling just for a few moments. For example, if you picked "sweating" then focus your entire attention now on just noticing how sweaty you are feeling in this moment.

Great! Now, we are going to imagine that you took this sensation to the dog park and took the leash off. That means that just for a few moments, we are only going to focus on this sensation while allowing it to be here, allowing it to be as strong or as weak as it needs to be.

If you are willing, I'm going to ask you to close your eyes and focus only on this one sensation. Fully allow it to be here, allow yourself to feel this way.

Ready?

Go!

How did it go? What did you notice? Did you find you could put up with focusing just on this sensation?

Would you be willing to try another one?

See if you can focus on each of these sensations one at a time for at least 1 to 2 minutes.

What did you notice as time went on? Write or draw in the box below.

The more we can let our emotions "off the leash," one bit at a time, the easier it can be for us to face these emotions as time goes on.

The Valve exercise for anxiety, anger, trauma, and grief

Another variation of this activity is The Valve, which can also be helpful for assisting clients with mindfulness, as well as the willingness to feel uncomfortable sensations and emotions, such as anxiety, anger, trauma trigger, or grief.

The Valve

Have you ever seen an air mattress? Or perhaps bicycle tires or a beach ball? Each of these has a little valve, which allows the air to be pumped in, as well as to be let out. In a similar way, we can practice letting some of the pressure or tension out of our body.

Take a few moments to notice any areas in your body where you might feel tense, such as in your shoulders, your jaw, your chest, your stomach, your forehead, or the top of your head.

Imagine that each of these areas has a little valve that you can open to allow some of the pressure out. If possible, see if you can actually pretend to open a valve in these parts of your body, one at a time. Each time you open a valve to let some of the pressure out, see if you can sit back and breathe for a few moments, allowing your body to settle as you are practicing this exercise.

Many people have a difficult time acknowledging their own victories and frequently only focus on their own struggles as a way of criticizing themselves. In fact, to an outside observer, the many challenges that our clients might be going through demonstrate the incredible amount of resilience that our clients have. For example, many teens and young adults with anxiety and depression report struggling with getting out of bed in the morning, which also correlates with higher levels of the stress hormone, cortisol, in their saliva (Heaney, Phillips, and Carroll, 2010).

Analyzing the typical cortisol patterns throughout the day, we know that cortisol levels are typically highest in the morning and lowest before evening bedtime (Hucklebridge, Clow, and Evans, 1998). Given that many people who are struggling with depression and anxiety experience higher cortisol levels as stress, this means that getting out of bed is the most stressful thing that people do every day! This means that the mere act of getting out of bed is already a victory.

The following activity is designed to help clients to realize that their success is determined by what they do, not by how they feel. In fact, if they are able to battle some of their monsters and still show up to school or work, that is already a major win in their battlefield.

Counting Your Dragons

Some people just get up and go to work or school. Others have to fight a whole bunch of dragons just to get here. Dragons are any challenges that we might face, such as struggling to get out of bed, feeling tired, feeling anxious, sad, or lonely, having to interact with people we don't like, or having to do things we don't want to do. Each one of these challenges is a dragon.

Imagine that you are fighting off two or maybe even three or four dragons at the same time with one hand, while trying to do your work with another. It would make sense then that it would take you longer to complete your work or that it might not be as well done as if you were not facing a large group of dragons. Having the understanding of how much you are already able to accomplish on a daily basis makes a difference.

So, let's count your dragons. How many dragons did you already fight today? What were they? Write or draw your answer.

Wow! That's impressive!! Take a moment to celebrate yourself. You are a warrior!

As we begin to take down some of the defences and armours that the client has spent many years building, what they might discover behind these internal fences might surprise them. Behind the walls of anger, resentment, anxiety, and frustration is often the most innocent form of vulnerability—the desire to be loved and accepted. The desire for love and belonging is the oldest most universal human need (Brown, 2015) and when it is not met, it can lead to pain (physical and emotional), as well as anger, shame, panic attacks, and (in some cases) isolation.

Sometimes, the pain of not having their needs met is so excruciating that our clients might not be able to realize that just as they are hurting, the people around them might be hurting too, and hence, might react unkindly. There is an expression, "Hurt people hurt people." What it means is that people who are hurting and suffering might be more likely, at least in some cases, to be less compassionate, and less understanding toward others. However, what happens when they try to communicate from a vulnerable perspective? Many people might believe that if they communicate from a gentle, open, vulnerable perspective, they will be disrespected or not taken seriously. However, when people are able to openly communicate with others about how they feel and what they need, they are more likely to be heard and more likely to have their needs met.

Here is an activity to illustrate this practice (versions for older children/teens/adults, and for younger children). You might need to assist children with these exercises, such as by writing in the thought and speech bubbles and providing them with options for how to respond to different situations.

These worksheets can also be used as homework practice.

Injured Talk vs. Courageous Talk for Teens/Adults

Injured talk is what we say, or do, when someone we care about says or does something that hurts us, or connects with our fear, or other deep emotions.

Injured talk can feel like a personal attack and we can feel like we have to fight to defend ourselves. Reacting with injured talk can make us lose sight of what is actually important to us and is less likely to enable us to have our needs met. Injured talk often presents as blame or defensiveness, in which case both people are not able to really hear each other to meet each other's needs.

Courageous talk is being vulnerable about our fears, our insecurities, and our hopes. It involves letting other people know how we feel and what we need from a vulnerable (non-blaming) perspective. Courageous talk also includes setting boundaries, even when the other person may react or dislike what we are saying or doing. Courageous talk comes from the place inside of us where we are able to step back a little, take a breath, and listen to ourselves and to what is important to us.

Here is an example of what injured talk might look like. Notice that what the monsters say points to them feeling angry or frustrated with one another. But when we actually see their thought bubbles, we see that their anger and frustration comes from the place of hurt and fear.

Let's think of a scenario in which you had an argument with a friend or family member. In the speech bubbles, write in what was actually said in the argument. In the thought bubbles, write in what you might have been thinking on a deeper, more vulnerable level. See if you can also add what your friend/family member might have been thinking and feeling if we assume that they might have been feeling vulnerable too.

What might be some of the things you wish you could help your friend or family member to understand?

_____

_____

_____

_____

Let's assume that your friend/family member acted unkindly not because they don't care about you, but rather because they are hurt. What do you think they might be feeling and needing at that time? What can you do to support them and also to express how you feel?

_____

_____

_____

_____

☆

Injured Talk vs. Courageous Talk for Kids

Sometimes, when someone is not listening to what we want or is not being fair we might get upset or angry. Sometimes we might think that the person is doing this on purpose and that they don't care about us. We might even shout at them and call them names. When we act this way, we are using our *injured talk*.

Injured talk is what we say or do when someone says or does something that hurts our feelings. We might think that this person is hurting us on purpose. So, we might yell at them or ignore them.

Unfortunately, injured talk is usually very hurtful to other people and will end up making things worse instead of better.

Courageous talk is superhero talk. It means being open about how we feel and what we want.

In the picture below is an example of what injured talk might look like. Notice that what the monsters say shows how angry they are at one another. But when we see their thought bubbles, we see that their anger actually comes from feeling hurt and scared.

Now, let's try a practice exercise. Using the blank thought and speech bubbles below, let's think of what you could say to your friend or family member to help them understand how you feel and what you need. We can also think about how they feel and what they need.

What might be some of the things you wish your friend or family member could understand? Think about what hurt you and what you need from them. You can say these out loud.

Let's assume that your friend or family member said or did something wrong not because they don't care about you, but because they are hurt. What do you think they might be feeling and needing at that time? What can you do to support them and also to express how you feel?

Savoring practices

Although many mindfulness practices focus on noticing (and accepting) negative or neutral body sensations and experiences, it is just as important to focus on mindfully noticing the pleasant experiences. Practices related to mindfulness, which specifically focus on enjoying the moment and prolonging this experience, are called savoring practices (Kiken, Lundberg, and Fredrickson *et al.*, 2017). Savoring practices could include purposely paying attention to the taste of a delicious meal, noticing a sweet or otherwise enjoyable moment, or recalling a sweet memory. The ability to practice mindfulness by practicing awareness of positive emotions can potentially increase mood and resilience against unpleasant events or emotions (Kiken *et al.*, 2017).

The following two activities provide examples of how to guide the client through mindful savoring practices.

Savoring Foods

When Harry Potter learns about Dementors—terrible monsters that are said to suck the happiness out of people—he learns that chocolate can help people to regain their energy after such an attack.

In fact, there is some truth to that because certain foods, such as chocolate, can sometimes make us feel better. However, it is not the food itself that has this ability, it is how we consume it.

Sometimes, we can eat our favorite food or drink and barely notice that we ate or drank it. This often happens when we are distracted, such as when we are also watching TV, or talking to someone, or playing a game. When we are not paying attention to what we are eating or drinking, we might not be able to notice how truly magical the food or drink might taste or smell.

If you are able to taste or smell food, see if you can select your favorite thing to eat (such as chocolate or another snack) or your favorite thing to drink (such as hot chocolate or tea, for example).

Imagine that you have never tasted this food or drink before. Imagine that it is magical in some ways. See if you can notice the way this food or drink looks. Does it feel warm or cold to the touch? See if you can smell it as if you've never smelled it before. What does it smell like? See if you can take a small bite or sip. Slowly and gently. And enjoy.

What did you notice?

_____

_____

_____

_____

_____

_____

_____

_____

_____

_____

_____

Sometimes, we might be so caught up in our own anxiety or daily stressors that we might have a difficult time noticing the truly wonderful events that are happening in that moment. At other times, we might actually notice the magic of a loving moment and it can take our breath away.

It happened several years ago. My husband and I were in Germany for a talk I was scheduled to give in Hamburg. I had everything planned out. We were going to get to Hamburg by 5pm (17:00) and then I would have 2 hours to practice for my presentation, then we would have dinner, go to bed, wake up at 6am, and be on our way.

However, when we arrived in Frankfurt for our layover to Hamburg, we found out that our flight was canceled. I started to panic, but my husband was able to find someone to help us to arrange to board the next flight, which would leave two hours later. In my mind, I redid the math—we would arrive by 7pm (19:00), I would prepare for a few hours, then have a late dinner, then go to bed, and still be able to wake up at 6am to be on our way for my talk.

As we lined up to board the plane, there was an announcement that all flights in and out of Frankfurt were canceled for the rest of the day due to thunderstorms. Immediately, lines to talk to attendants began to fill. I was feeling extremely distressed. I had never missed a talk I was supposed to give. I did not wish to be irresponsible. I didn't know what to do.

Thankfully, my husband again found us someone who could help. The kind attendant put us on a train to Hamburg, which would get us there by midnight. However, the train would be leaving in 15 minutes on the other side of the airport.

Running through the airport with our luggage, we just made it to the train. As it started moving, I began to relax. The beautiful scenery with castles, old churches, and rivers looked like something out of a fantasy book. I opened my laptop and began reviewing my presentation, realizing that we would have to go straight to sleep once we arrived at our hotel.

Two hours into our journey, the train stopped. Then there was an announcement in German. Then everyone around us started yelling. We finally found someone who could explain the situation to us—there was a fire on the train tracks and the train would have to wait.

Two and a half hours later, the train began to move backwards. We found out that the train had to turn back in order to go around the fire.

It was 3:30am by the time we got to our hotel. Two and a half hours later, exhausted, hungry, sleep deprived, and extremely jet lagged with a 9-hour time difference, we made it to my talk.

I felt truly grateful to be there and to have been able to arrive on time, something I highly value. During lunchtime, all the attendees went out and my husband and I were alone. He brought me a latte, the most amazing latte I have ever had. I looked over at him and smiled. It was just the two of us, enjoying a quiet moment together. The light summer breeze was both gentle and kind. And I realized in that moment with tears in my eyes how powerful this moment was. Throughout the chaos, my partner, the love of my life, was right there by my side. We smiled at one another and held hands. To this day, that moment brings tears to my eyes and warms my heart. I knew right there and then that it was a truly special moment.

When it comes to savoring practices, we can savor our past memories or we can savor our current experiences. This means noticing in that very moment that *this is that sweet savoring moment happening right now.* And when you can notice that, it can be truly magical.

Savoring Moments

Sometimes we go through life not really noticing when we feel happy, mostly only noticing when we feel sad, angry, or scared. However, noticing sweet moments when they occur and remembering our favorite memories can make us feel better when we are going through a hard time.

Can you think of a memory of an event where you felt truly happy? It could be a big event, such as a birthday party, or a small event, such as laughing with the people you love the most. Perhaps you were playing a game with your best friend or maybe you were enjoying your time with your pet. Or maybe you were reading your favorite book or watching your favorite movie.

See if you can write or draw that memory with as many details as possible.

Over the next few weeks, see if you notice moments when you are feeling happy. When you notice those moments, silently remind yourself, "This is that happy moment happening right now."

Many of your clients might have forgotten how to smile. They might not be able to see in this moment that there is a light at the end of the dark forest, that there is hope. Remember that your kindness, compassion, and encouragement are exactly what your clients need in their darkest moments. Remember that you are making a difference. Thank you for making this world a better place.

Chapter 6

SELF-COMPASSION CHARM

Have you ever really needed to talk to someone about what you were going through, only to mindlessly go through your contacts, wondering if any of your friends would actually understand you? Many of our clients are struggling with that notion on a daily basis. Many feel incredibly alone, sometimes more so when they are around people who don't seem to be experiencing the same kinds of struggles. However, such perceived loneliness can place the individual at a higher risk of developing cardiovascular problems; a higher risk of developing (or faster progression of) Alzheimer's Disease; increased mental health pathology including depression, anxiety, suicidal ideation or attempts; as well as suppressed anti-inflammatory gene expression and increased pro-inflammatory gene expression, and higher risk of mortality in older adults... (Cacioppo, Fowler, and Christakis, 2009; Epel and Lithgow, 2014).

The detrimental effects of loneliness point to the crucial human need for belonging. In fact, a sense of belonging has the inverse health effects to those of perceived loneliness (Øverup *et al.*, 2017; Van Dam *et al.*, 2011; Xu and Roberts, 2010). One speculation as to why this is the case is that perceived loneliness often leads to higher depression rates, coupled with a sense of perceived burdensomeness, which can lead to social isolation and a disconnection to one's sense of purpose. These factors can put the individual at higher risk for depression and suicide (Øverup *et al.*, 2017). On the other hand, perceived belonging has been shown to reduce depression and loneliness, as well as overall wellbeing (Øverup *et al.*, 2017).

Given that human belonging is essential for most human beings' wellbeing, it can be especially alarming that many people struggling with anxiety, depression, and PTSD are more likely to self-isolate when they are struggling than to reach out for help. This is especially alarming since depression, anxiety, and social isolation pose as risk factors for mortality in patients who experience medical problems, such as heart failure (Friedmann *et al.*, 2006). A meta-analysis of 300,000 patients found that social isolation (or perceived social isolation) poses as high a mortality risk to an individual as chronic alcohol abuse and smoking. And since loneliness is the new smoking, then it seems imperative that our clients are able to find sources of support and social connection when they need it most.

Finding a fictional friend when feeling lonely

In order to assess participants' willingness to seek social connections, researchers interviewed 1199 college students who were asked about their trauma experiences and their loneliness levels, as well as their connections with classmates and social surrogates, such as fictional characters from TV shows, books, or films (Gabriel *et al.*, 2017). The results of the study indicated that college students who were exposed to trauma were more likely to report turning toward a social surrogate (e.g., a character from a TV show, book, or film) than participants without trauma. Furthermore, those who were exposed to trauma were also more likely to be drawn to social surrogates when feeling lonely, as compared to participants who did not experience trauma. In addition, participants who experienced trauma were more likely to report increased feelings of social connection when writing about a social surrogate than when writing a control essay (e.g., when asked to describe the objects in their room; Gabriel *et al.*, 2017). Similar benefits of increased feelings of social belonging were also found after participants experienced rejection or heartbreak (Derrick *et al.*, 2009).

The following activity can be done with clients who are feeling lonely, rejected, or heartbroken.

Introduce Your Best Friend

Sometimes when we are having a bad day, or when we are feeling sad, bored, or lonely, we might feel alone, even if other people are in the same room. In these situations, it can sometimes help to think of your best friend. Your best friend could be a friend that you care about and spend a lot of time with. Or your best friend could be your favorite family member, or even a pet. Your best friend could also be your favorite character, for example, Batman, Wonder Woman, Harry Potter, or Dean Winchester (from *Supernatural*).

In the space below, please write about your best friend (or draw them) in as much detail as possible. Describe them, what you do together or what you would like to do together (for example, watching a movie together), and also what you like about them.

Interestingly, although people with PTSD and those who were exposed to trauma but did not develop PTSD both reported being more likely to engage in social surrogacy when feeling lonely, the actual benefits (i.e., the feeling of connection) following this interaction were not observed in participants who were exhibiting high PTSD symptomatology (Gabriel *et al.*, 2017). One possible explanation for this discrepancy is that individuals with PTSD, as well as individuals with depression and anxiety, are likely to be highly self-critical (Øverup *et al.*, 2017; Thompson and Waltz, 2008). One possible reason for that is that creating emotional barriers, including high levels of self-criticism, might create an artificial sense of emotional safety after exposure to trauma. However, research studies demonstrate that self-compassion can help individuals to better manage anxiety, depression, and trauma symptoms, as well as to find a sense of emotional safety in seeking social support and connection (Maheux and Price, 2016; Thompson and Waltz, 2008).

Taken together, these findings can be interpreted to mean that although social connection may be the ideal resiliency factor for helping individuals manage their mental (and physical) health, social surrogacy may provide some support for individuals when social support may be unavailable. Furthermore, self-compassion may provide the key to strengthening the individual's sense of emotional resilience and emotional safety in order to allow the individual to build meaningful social connections (Neff and Dahm, 2015).

Self-compassion as emotional safety

Opening up to the idea of facing the kind of emotional and physical pain (the monsters) that our clients have been running away from can seem like the most impossible of all tasks. However, one of the main hesitations clients have against facing their internal monsters is usually that they might not believe themselves capable of being able to "handle" such an exposure. If, however, the client were to be able to learn specific tools for easing their suffering while facing their challenges (e.g., self-compassion), they might not only be more willing to face their symptoms, they might actually feel more empowered by these practices (Waite, Knight, and Lee, 2015).

Self-compassion refers to offering ourselves the same kind of compassion, understanding, and kindness as we would toward a dear friend, a favorite family member, or a pet (Neff and Dahm, 2015; Neff and Germer, 2018). Essentially, self-compassion is not meant to "take away" our suffering, but rather to be a supportive and soothing factor for when suffering is present. Self-compassion teaches us to turn toward our suffering, with the understanding that suffering is universal and expected, and with taking a kind approach toward ourselves (Neff and Dahm, 2015). Self-compassion has been shown to be helpful for people struggling with depression, anxiety, PTSD, psychosis, addiction, chronic pain, and other disorders (Maheux and Price, 2016; Neff and Dahm, 2015; Thompson and Waltz, 2008).

According to self-compassion pioneer, Kristin Neff, self-compassion consists of three elements: mindfulness, common humanity, and self-kindness (Neff and Dahm, 2015; Neff and Germer, 2018). Mindfulness refers to noticing our experience, such as the experience of depression, anxiety, traumatic memory, or an obsessive thought. The reason why this component is essential is because without being able to notice that we are suffering, we would not have the understanding that we are in need of self-compassion. This practice is the direct opposite to avoidance, suppression, and judgment of our emotions, which have been shown to be detrimental to our mental health (Thompson and Waltz, 2010).

The second component of self-compassion, common humanity, refers to recognizing that our experiences are universal. Common humanity might involve recognizing that everyone makes mistakes, that everyone feels lonely, frustrated, scared, or overwhelmed sometimes. For example, in this practice, the individual can remind themselves, "Just like me, other people all over the world might be struggling with loneliness too. Everyone thinks they are not good enough sometimes. Most people in my situation would feel the same way." This practice is the direct opposite of self-pity, which tends to assume that the individual is alone in their suffering and that no one else could understand them or relate to them.

The final element of self-compassion is self-kindness, which refers to treating ourselves with the same degree of kindness as we would have toward someone we truly love and care about, such as a dear friend, a favorite family member, or a pet. Many individuals are kind and patient with others, while being overly harsh (and sometimes unrealistic) regarding their expectations of themselves. Self-kindness encourages people to put themselves in the same kind regard as they would have toward a loved one, for example, by providing themselves with the permission to rest and eat, giving themselves a hug, or talking to themselves in a kind manner (Neff and Dahm, 2015).

The two activities that follow were created to help clients understand the basic self-compassion elements and skills.

Compassion Toward a Hero

Everyone goes through a hard time sometimes. Batman, Superman, and Wonder Woman have all lost people they loved and cared about. Every person, real and fictional, feels sad, scared, or overwhelmed sometimes.

I'd like you to think of a superhero or another fictional character that has ever felt sad or scared. What was going on in that situation? Write about it or draw it in the space below.

Can you name the emotions that character was going through (either out loud or by writing them down)?

What would you say to this character in the situation if you could actually talk to them in that situation? Write about it or draw your response in the space below.

Have you ever known anyone else who also felt similar emotions as this character has felt? If yes, imagine that you could say something to support that person. What would you say?

Do you ever feel that way? Do you ever experience similar emotions—feeling sad, scared, or overwhelmed? If so, what do you think you could say to yourself in the same caring way that you treated your friend and the superhero you wrote about? Write about it or draw your response in the space below.

Self-Compassion Potion

Like Harry Potter, we too can learn some magic. Believe it or not, we can learn ways of discovering our inner sense of magical abilities through connecting with our emotions. And, just like some of the magical lessons Harry Potter and his friends learn at Hogwarts, we can also learn to find the magic within our emotional experiences.

All emotions that we feel are necessary and informative. They tell us what we are feeling and what we need. Our emotions are the root of our magical potential and if we learn how to use them, we can learn how to help our hearts and souls to heal.

Our bodies have the capability to create a magical potion, of sorts—a hormone called *oxytocin,* which can help to transform our painful emotions, like sadness, fear, and loneliness into easier ones, which include love and compassion.

Here is how to activate this magical potion:

Step 1: Noticing

For this part of the exercise, take a few minutes to sit still and just notice how you are feeling, almost as if tuning into your Spidey senses. Just notice how and what you are feeling. Notice the sensations in your chest and stomach, since that's where most of our emotions live. Notice if you are feeling sad, angry, frustrated, scared, worried, excited, or any other emotions. Notice where in your body you are feeling these emotions and how you are experiencing them. Just notice these sensations for a few minutes. Breathe. Remind yourself that this might be *that* difficult moment that you experience from time to time. Is there a word or a phrase you can say to yourself as a reminder? Perhaps something like this: "This is one of those difficult moments. It's happening right now. I feel scared, sad, and alone. I've felt this way before."

Write down what you might be able to say to yourself during difficult moments to notice and acknowledge your experience:

_____

_____

_____

_____

Step 2: Just like me

Take a few moments to recognize that just like you, millions of people are also feeling this way right now in this very moment. Millions of people are also sad, scared, angry, anxious, worried, overwhelmed, or bored. Your experience is perfectly normal, completely understandable, and anyone in your situation would feel the same way.

Remind yourself that just like you, your favorite hero, real or fictional, has also dealt with a lot of similar struggles. For example, "I'm feeling very alone right now, like Harry Potter has felt," or "I'm feeling a lot of grief and sadness right now, just like Batman has felt."

Write out what you might say to yourself to remind you that you are not alone in this experience.

_____

_____

_____

_____

Step 3: Be kind

In the same way as you would be kind toward another person who is going through the same experience, in the same way as Dumbledore would be kind to Harry, or any other students, see if you can find kindness toward yourself. Try placing your arms around yourself to give you a hug, hug a pillow, or gently press on your heart centre with both hands. All of these actions can release the oxytocin chemical into your body. This chemical can help you heal, can help you to find peace when you are struggling, like a hug from a dear friend.

Notice what you need. Notice if you need a hug, or to rest, or to be reassured, and see if there is any way that you can support yourself in the very way that you need. Because you are magical.

Write out something you might say to yourself in this situation next time you are feeling this way. If it is too challenging to think about something kind you might say to yourself, think about something kind you would like to say to your favorite hero if they were in the same situation or something kind that your hero would say to you—for instance, "You didn't deserve what happened to you. You didn't deserve to be treated that way. I see your pain and you are not alone. I care about you and we will get through this together."

_____

_____

_____

_____

_____

As mentioned in the Self-Compassion Potion activity above, self-compassion practices have been shown to lead to higher levels of oxytocin in the body (Bellosta-Batalla *et al.*, 2020). Oxytocin is a neuropeptide secreted by the hypothalamus. Oxytocin can actually function both as a hormone and as a neurotransmitter (a neurological signal). Oxytocin is involved in soothing others, self-soothing, trust and social bonding, emotional and sexual intimacy, and stress buffering, as well as perspective taking and empathy (Bellosta-Batalla *et al.*, 2020). Higher oxytocin can support the formation of steady social connections and prosocial behaviors, often leading to reduced anxiety and distress (Crespi, 2016).

It seems that the three self-compassion elements—mindfulness, common humanity, and self-kindness—are the key for many people's emotional wellbeing. For instance, Chanteil, a well-known *Harry Potter* fanfiction writer, shares that when she was growing up, she was placed in foster care in which she was abused, isolated, and shamed. Chanteil reports that at one point the abuse had become so bad that she considered suicide. However, her ability to notice her own emotional distress (mindfulness), to realize that she was just like Harry Potter, that just like him she was also going through abuse and emotional pain (common humanity) meant that she was able to find kindness toward herself (self-kindness) to support herself through that horrific time of her life (Scarlet, 2017).

Although the extensive research related to self-compassion shows a vast plethora of physical and emotional benefits of this practice (Bluth and Neff, 2018), many might struggle with it, as they might believe practicing self-compassion to be selfish. Interestingly, research studies find the opposite results— practicing self-compassion provides opportunity for empathy and compassion toward others (Neff and Germer, 2018). In rebuilding our own inner strength, recharging our own battery, we can be more emotionally present for other people. This finding does not only apply to our clients. This also applies to us, the clinicians. The ability to support ourselves by attending to our own physical and emotional needs can offer us the resilience that we need to reduce emotional burnout and to better attend to our clients, especially when we are experiencing empathic distress. Empathic distress refers to a concern for the wellbeing of others and a severe distress when seeing them suffering. Empathic distress often occurs due to emotional exhaustion or lack of self-compassion (Klimecki and Singer, 2012). The following self-compassion exercise is intended to help people struggling with empathic distress. It is a variation of Kristin Neff's and Chris Germer's (2018) Compassionate Breathing In and Out exercise (for more information, I highly recommend their book, *The Mindful Self-Compassion Workbook: A Proven Way to Accept Yourself, Build Inner Strength, and Thrive*). This exercise is one I like to use myself and one I also use with my clients. Use this as the basis for a script when working with the client/clients.

Magical Breathing

Sometimes, we might see someone we care about going through something very painful. For example, we might see a dear friend fall down and get hurt or we might see someone crying because they lost their dog, or perhaps because their family member passed away.

Seeing other people in physical or emotional pain can be painful for us as well. There's a reason for that—we hurt because we care. Our heart hurts because that's what it was designed to do. When we love someone, we hurt when they hurt. However, this pain can also happen when we see someone we don't know who might be suffering. In this case, it might be our love for humanity, for animals, for living beings that is causing us to feel this way.

There is an exercise we can use to soothe our own pain and in order to be able to support others who are struggling. This exercise is called "Magical Breathing." It is called that because through the practice of compassionate breathing our body creates certain chemicals that can help to soothe our emotional pain, potentially allowing us to then help others.

In order to try Magical Breathing, find a comfortable position, ideally sitting down, if that is possible.

Breathe in.

Imagine that each time you are breathing in, you are breathing in healing magic. Imagine breathing in this magic through your nose or mouth, and then imagine it spreading all through your body. Healing you. Offering you much needed love, kindness, and support.

And then breathe out.

Imagine that each time you are breathing out, you are sending that healing magic toward the person or animal that is suffering, whether you know them or whether you have never met them. Imagine them being embraced in healing magic from your body to theirs.

Breathe in magic for yourself. Feel yourself bathed in warm, healing, magical light.

Breathe out magic for another. Imagine them soothed and healed by your magic.

Continue this practice as long as you need to and whenever you need to, and know that this practice is not only helping you, it is also helping others around you.

Managing burnout

One of the possible causes, as well as outcomes, of empathic distress is emotional burnout. Burnout refers to physical and/or emotional exhaustion, which can lead to both psychological and physiological issues. Burnout symptoms can include reduced concern for oneself or others, mistakes in the work setting, mistakes while driving or operating heavy machinery, irritability, frustration, impatience, lethargy, reduced job satisfaction, interpersonal conflicts, sleep problems, mental fog, dizziness and balance issues, frequent illness (such as the flu), inflammatory illnesses and flare-ups, as well as anxiety, depression and/or suicidal thoughts, cardiovascular disease, and premature death (Ahola *et al.*, 2010; Melamed *et al.*, 2006).

Self-compassion has been shown to be a potential resiliency factor against burnout and empathic distress (Beaumont *et al.*, 2016). The activity that follows is intended to help clients learn about ways to "recharge their own battery" as a way of building emotional resilience against burnout.

Recharge Your Battery

What do people do when their phone battery dies? I imagine that most people plug it in to recharge.

In a very similar way, we also sometimes need to "recharge" our own strength. Sometimes we might feel exhausted, scared, or alone when facing different challenges and might need a little break to do something relaxing or fun. Taking some time to look after ourselves when we are feeling tired, sad, angry, scared, or overwhelmed is called *self-compassion*.

Some people think that practicing self-compassion is selfish and that we should only do things for ourselves after we have completed our chores, our work, or other responsibilities. But scientists are finding that when we are not feeling well, taking a little self-care break can actually boost our energy to return to the tasks we have to complete.

Think about Superman. Superman is one of the most powerful superheroes of all time. But *kryptonite* can harm him. This is a substance from his home planet that can weaken his powers. To recharge his powers, Superman must fly toward the Earth's yellow sun. Once he has recharged, Superman can return to saving people once more.

In the same way, when Batman is injured, he sometimes needs to spend some time in his Batcave in order to rest and heal. Imagine what would happen to Batman if he continued to fight the Joker when he is injured, starving, or exhausted. Just like you, Batman needs to recharge his energy so that he can be the hero that he is.

When our own energy is running low, we might sometimes also need to rest. This might mean doing something to unwind and relax, such as playing a game, watching an episode of a fun television show, messaging a friend, drawing, or sleeping. This practice is not selfish, it is necessary, so that when we are done, we can have the energy that we need to be able to complete our other responsibilities.

Take a few moments and think about which activities would help you to recharge your battery when you are feeling tired, sad, angry, or overwhelmed:

- playing a video game for 30 minutes
- watching one episode of my favorite TV show
- talking with a friend for 30 minutes
- coloring or drawing for 30 minutes
- spending time with a family member or a pet
- reading one chapter of a fun book
- watching fun videos online for 30 minutes
- having a tasty hot drink, like tea or hot chocolate

- eating a snack
- napping for 30 minutes
- getting a hug
- other _____

These activities are not meant to become something that keeps you away from completing your work. They are meant to allow you to take a break so you can return to the important tasks you are working on afterwards.

On the lines below, write the task that you intend to return to after you are done recharging your batteries (for example, doing the dishes, your homework, or a report).

_____
_____
_____
_____
_____
_____
_____
_____

The Batcave sanctuary

Kids and adults alike can sometimes benefit from having a "Batcave"—a sanctuary of sorts, a safe place to go to when they are feeling overwhelmed, triggered, angry, or frustrated. For kids, it can be a cardboard cut-out house in the corner of their bedroom, for example. For teens and adults, the Batcave could be a specific corner of the room, perhaps blocked off by a curtain.

The idea of a Batcave is to allow the client to have a space to go to for emotion regulation in which they can have privacy and practice self-soothing techniques. For child clients, it is very important that the family members understand that when their child is in their Batcave, they should be allowed their space and privacy. The same condition applies to teen and adult clients.

Inside the Batcave, the client could have tools that could help them to self-soothe, such as pillows, selected pictures, stuffed animals, coloring books, comic books, or other favorite books. It might include twinkling lights, a snack, or a music player. The hope is that the individual would be able to elect to go into their Batcave as a way of practicing self-compassion when they are feeling overwhelmed to reduce interpersonal conflicts and increase emotion regulation skills. As therapists, we can help the client to consider which items they would like to include in their Batcave, when they would like to go into it, and encourage discussion with the family members to allow them to understand the client's need for privacy when in the Batcave.

Build Your Own Batcave

In order to rest, have some peace of mind, and heal, Superman sometimes goes to the Fortress of Solitude. After spending some time there, he appears stronger and more powerful once again.

In the same way, when he is injured or tired, Batman returns to his Batcave to rest, heal, and recover.

If you could design your own Batcave, your own space where you can go to spend some time to rest and relax, what would it look like? What items would be in that place? Perhaps books, games, pillows, coloring books would be there, or maybe your dog or cat would also accompany you in there?

Write out your description of your own Batcave or draw it in the box.

What might be some of the situations in which you'd like to go to your Batcave? For example, after a fight with a family member, or when you're feeling stressed, overwhelmed, or scared. You can either write these situations out or say them out loud.

_____

_____

_____

_____

_____

_____

_____

_____

_____

What might some of the rules for your Batcave be? For example, no one is allowed in there except for you.

_____

_____

_____

_____

_____

_____

_____

_____

_____

_____

This Batcave is your safe space. You are allowed to go in there any time you wish.

Managing perfectionism

In addition to burnout and emotional distress, another situation in which self-compassion can be extremely beneficial is when someone makes a mistake. Most people are highly critical of themselves and those raised in critical households, as well as individuals struggling with anxiety, depression, eating disorders, or PTSD, are likely to be extremely self-critical (Neff and Germer, 2018). Perfectionism and self-shaming can be thought of as one's heartfelt desire for love and belonging, fueled by terror of rejection and disconnection. When we are caught in the cycle of perfectionism, we miss our opportunity for connection and creativity.

Making Mistakes Gamefully

How do you react when you've made a mistake? Do you try to correct it? Do you avoid thinking about it? Do you get angry with yourself or anyone else?

Sometimes, when we make a mistake we might even shame ourselves, and call ourselves names or tell ourselves off.

But the truth is that everyone makes mistakes sometimes. In fact, that is how we learn. If we never make mistakes, we never learn what works and what doesn't work. If we never fall, we never learn to lift ourselves up.

By striving to be perfect, we might be missing out on important learning opportunities. You see, perfectionism is the death of creativity. To be creative, you need to allow yourself to make mistakes.

Think of making mistakes like playing a video game. With each level that you play, you will face more and more challenges. It makes sense that when you encounter challenges that you have never faced before, you might make a mistake. It makes sense that sometimes if you're playing when you are tired or hungry you might make a mistake, and that if you're facing a very big monster boss in the game, you might not defeat him on the first try.

Think of each setback as information, something that gives you XP (experience) points, so that you can come back, level up, and keep going.

If you are willing, please write down a little reminder for yourself below, something kind and supportive you can say to yourself in the future when you have made a mistake. See if you can think of it like learning to play a new game—expecting that you won't be playing perfectly and being able to enjoy the game all the same.

_____

_____

_____

_____

_____

_____

_____

_____

_____

  129

Since many clients utilize gaming as a form of self-compassion practices, I wanted to briefly discuss the Superhero Therapy stance on gaming, including video games, phone app games, computer games, table-top games, role-playing games and others. Although there has been a lot of controversy about video games specifically, research studies actually find tremendous benefits of games, including improvement to coordination and concentration skills, problem-solving skills, and social skills (Granic, Lobel, and Engels, 2014; Sutton-Smith, 1999). Another study found that playing phone app games such as *Bejeweled* mimicked the benefits of mindfulness by helping the players increase their heart rate variability (HRV), reducing anxiety and depression, improving positive emotions, and improving distress tolerance after a setback (Russoniello, O'Brien, and Parks, 2009; Russoniello, Fish, and O'Brien, 2013), as well as reducing PTSD symptomatology (Holmes *et al.*, 2009) and reducing preoperative anxiety in children (Lee *et al.*, 2013).

Concern about gaming

Unfortunately, many gamers are faced with a lot of criticism from their family members, teachers, and (on occasion) their mental health providers. Many gamers are shamed by being told to "do something real" and "stop wasting time." However, what many people fail to realize is that games have many functions. For many people, games function as a way to socially connect with faraway friends and family members. For others, games function as a way of unwinding and de-stressing, in other words, as a way of practicing self-compassion when they are otherwise struggling. For some, games are essentially a sport—they might play on a team and compete in a tournament. In fact, gaming and game development are some of the largest growing career paths for young people and some universities offer full scholarships to advanced video gamers, in a similar way as they do for star athletes. For more information about the psychological benefits of gaming, check out Jane McGonigal's book, *SuperBetter* (McGonigal, 2015).

I've had many concerned parents, teachers, and therapists ask me something along the lines of, "My child plays eight hours per day. How do I get him to stop?" I often then ask the concerned adult which game the child is playing, only to be met with, "I honestly have no idea. I never asked."

To ask about the game the person is playing is the most essential question we can ask when working with clients who like to play games. Chances are, they have already been shamed, questioned, and misunderstood. The best thing we can do is to find out more about the game(s) they are playing and the function of these games for that individual.

The worksheet below is intended to help the provider to better understand the function of the client's gaming behavior (e.g., anxiety management, self-care, social connection, e-sport, etc.), as well as to assist the client with figuring out a way to use the game as a self-compassion (but not avoidance) practice. For small children, the therapist can fill out the worksheet and use it as an information-gathering resource. Older clients can fill it out themselves.

Games Power Up

I know that games can be a lot of fun and many of us like to play them both for fun and also to help us feel better when we feel sad, angry, or anxious. So, let's focus on the games that you like to play.

Which games do you like to play? What is your favorite game?

_____

_____

_____

What do you like about this game?

_____

_____

_____

Is this a single player or a multiplayer game?

_____

_____

_____

Who do you usually play with?

_____

_____

_____

How often do you play?

_____

How do you play it? What do you have to do in order to win?

_____

_____

_____

_____

☆

What is your character like in this game?

_____

_____

_____

What is it like when you win? How do you feel when you win?

_____

_____

_____

What is it like when you lose? What do you feel and what do you do when you lose?

_____

_____

_____

When are you most likely to play this game? (When bored, sad, scared, when friends play, etc.)

_____

_____

_____

What might be a way that we can use this game to help power you up when you are going through a hard time, so that you are still able to play and also do anything else that you need to do? (For example, maybe when you are having a bad day, you can play for 30 minutes, then do what you need to do, and then play some more later on.)

_____

_____

_____

_____

_____

☆

Too busy to practice self-compassion? No problem

One of the main barriers to many individuals' abilities to practice self-compassion is having a very busy schedule. Many believe that in order to practice self-compassion, they have to dedicate 45 to 60 minutes on a daily basis to some kind of a practice, often viewing it as yet another item on their already overpopulated to-do list. In order to assist clients with very hectic schedules, I have developed the Self-Compassion for the Busy exercise.

Self-Compassion for the Busy

I know, I know. Like the White Rabbit from Alice in Wonderland, you don't have time to add yet another item to your daily tasks. I know that you already have to break dozens of laws of physics in order to complete all your impossible to-do lists. Don't worry, nothing on this list will take much of your time, hardly any at all, but hopefully it will help to supercharge you for your already hectic schedule.

Here are some possible ways that you can practice self-compassion "on the go." Please circle the ones you'd be willing to try:

- Take a breath. Take one intentional breath while switching between tasks or appointments. This very brief mindfulness practice can help you to refocus and reduce fatigue.
- Every time you check the time on your phone, watch, or computer, check in with your body. Ask yourself, "Am I breathing or was I holding my breath? Am I tensing or relaxed? Am I hungry? Do I need to use the restroom?" Brief moments of this kind can alert you to what you need, remind you to breathe, eat, and take care of yourself in order to increase your productivity.
- Check your posture, including shoulder tension and jaw clenching, when you are driving, being driven, walking, or taking public transport. Any time you come to a stop, check your body. Are you leaning forward, as if trying to make your car or the tube go faster? Are you clenching your jaw? Are your shoulders raised close to your ears or are they relaxed? These kinds of check-ins can potentially help to reduce your muscle tension and headaches.

- See if you can do everything half a second slower—walk just a little bit slower, talk a little slower. It might seem like you are going at snail speed but actually, you're helping to manage your nervous system. When you are walking and talking quickly, your adrenaline surges, initially giving you additional energy, but over time, making you more tired and irritable. By moving and talking just a little bit slower, you are helping to balance your nervous system, so that you don't run out of energy. You will likely finish all your tasks in the same amount of time as if you were moving at your usual Flash-like speed.
- Pick one activity during the day, even if it only lasts 2–3 minutes, and do it mindfully, just for you. For example, see if you can eat at least one part of one of your meals slowly and mindfully to truly enjoy it. Or perhaps see if you can sip your tea or coffee in the morning for a few minutes in a slow, savoring, mindful way before you jump into the vortex of your day.

Know that no matter how busy you are, you deserve to be taken care of—you deserve to supercharge your inner battery.

Are monsters *really* monsters

In Chapter 2, we spent some time helping clients to identify their monsters—the unwanted internal experiences, including emotions, thoughts, sensations, and memories. Many clients come to therapy with the hope of getting rid of these unwanted experiences. Now that the client is learning about practicing compassion toward themselves and others, we can also offer them a new perspective: Are monsters *really* monsters? Or are they scary because we are scared and hurtful because we are hurt? What if monsters are actually just scared and defenceless beings, who simply don't know how to receive the support they so desperately need? The following activity offers an experiential practice for the client to work toward developing a sense of compassion toward their inner monsters. It combines elements of defusion practices from acceptance and commitment therapy (Hayes *et al.*, 2006) and self-compassion toward the inner-critic practices (Neff and Germer, 2018).

Compassion for the Monsters

We are so used to assuming that our internal monsters are "bad" and that we need to "make them go away" that we don't often stop to think about whether those monsters are actually monsters at all. Is it perhaps possible that they are scary because we are scared and hurtful because we are hurt? In other words, could the monsters be a representation of an injured part of us that really needs love and healing?

Let's try a brief writing exercise. First take a few moments to think about who your monsters are—perhaps you struggle with anxiety, depression, anger, or insecurity. Think about who your monsters are and what they are typically telling you. What are some of the messages they frequently send you?

_____

_____

_____

_____

_____

_____

Next, take a moment to consider that the monsters are not reacting this way out of malice but rather because they have some kind of an unmet need, such as the need for love, support, or emotional or physical safety.

Write down what your monsters might actually need when they are behaving this way.

_____

_____

_____

_____

_____

_____

Next, take a moment to imagine that perhaps they are actually trying to protect you from something but are not using the best strategies for doing so. For instance, your monsters could be trying to protect you from criticism by first criticizing you so harshly that no matter what anyone else says, it couldn't be as bad as what your monster says to you. Or perhaps your monsters are trying to protect you from rejection, heartbreak, or further pain? See if you can write down some possibilities of what your monsters might be trying to protect you from.

_____

_____

_____

_____

_____

_____

Now, see if you can thank the monsters for looking out for you and give them reassurance that you don't need their help any longer. For example, you can say, "Thanks, anxiety. I know you're trying to look out for me, but I've got it from here."

See if you can practice that in the space below:

_____

_____

_____

_____

_____

_____

This work may not be easy for the client and it might not be easy for you. And at the same time, I find that it is in the middle of our hardest work that sometimes the biggest changes happen. On the days that your own monsters might be telling you that you are not helping your clients or that you are not a good therapist (as mine are often telling me), may you always remember that the reason why you have those monsters in the first place is because you care. You care so much that you are going out of your way to learn additional skills and do additional trainings to help your clients. You think about how to help them not only in the session but between the sessions too. And your clients are thinking about what they've learned in between sessions too.

So, the next time that your monster makes you think that you are not good at what you do, I hope that you can thank your monster, all the while letting it know, "Thanks, I've got it from here." Because you do. You always have. Thank you for all that you do and all the times you have shown up even when it was difficult. You are the true definition of a hero.

Chapter 7
SENSE OF PURPOSE

THE HEROIC QUEST

What if I were to tell you that all the roads in your life have led you here? To a large degree, that's true. Your experiences, your desire to help people, your wanting to make a difference in this world have brought you to this line of work. But there could be something else too. For many of us, as providers, this journey is also about finding meaning after our own painful struggles.

Many people experiencing any sudden change in their health, such as a disability, sudden or gradual development of chronic pain, a new food allergy, or another health condition that affects the person's ability to complete their usual activities, can experience distress, anxiety, depression, grief over the change in their physical condition, and PTSD symptoms. Interestingly, disability and PTSD have the same development trajectories, suggesting that the two factors are related to one another (Sterling, Hendrikz, and Kenardy, 2011). However, meaning making has been shown to help people with chronic pain or other chronic health conditions to improve their overall functioning and reduce mental health symptomatology, and develop posttraumatic growth (Dezutter, Luyckx, and Wachholtz, 2015; Zeligman et al., 2018). It seems that when people with chronic physical or emotional pain engage in meaningful social and creative activities, such as dancing or

singing, their pain thresholds (their ability to tolerate pain) rise, while reducing their pain-related distress (Tarr, Launay, and Dunbar, 2016; Weinstein et al., 2016). Similar reductions in chronic physical and emotional pain are also seen in groups who focus on meaning making after experiencing a traumatic injury, such as a spinal cord injury (deRoon-Cassini et al., 2013).

I used to hate my migraines. Any time the weather would change, I would get blinding headaches that would bring me to my knees. I remember being sent home from school with debilitating migraines in elementary school. A neighbor, who saw me walking home on one of those occasions, looked mortified and helped me up the stairs and to my apartment, as I could barely put the key in the door. Before leaving, she said that there was something wrong with my eye. When I looked in the mirror, I saw that two blood vessels had popped in my right eye from the pain, making it appear bloody where the white space was supposed to be.

Over the years, I sought numerous remedies and heard hundreds of promises from experts who claimed that they would take away my migraines forever, and that I would be pain free if I were to stick with their regimen. Unfortunately, none of them worked. More unfortunately, I spent so much time chasing "the cure" that I neglected my own core values. I spent so much time being careful—not dancing, not listening to loud music, not traveling for the fear of getting sick with pain. And although I might have avoided a migraine or two, I was not living. Not really.

In college, I discovered dance and fell in love with the sport. I joined the dance team and then a social justice group. I started traveling and attending music concerts. I still had migraines but somehow they became less debilitating. The frequency and the intensity of them did not change but my experience of migraines did. In acceptance and commitment therapy terms, we could say that my *relationship* with my pain changed (Hayes, 2019). I found that living my life *with* my pain, as opposed to running away from it, allowed me to function better and to find a new sense of meaning.

To be honest, if I were to be offered a "magical cure" for my migraines now, I would

have to politely refuse. I have come to accept my migraines as a part of me. They have taught me to value pain-free days. They have taught me to appreciate my health and to develop compassion for others who are struggling with chronic illness. Most of all, they have given me a sense of purpose—by understanding chronic physical pain and the emotional pain that comes with it, I have found that my own priorities have shifted. I have found my inner strength; I have found a new sense of gratitude, and when I stopped running from my pain, I have also found myself. My pain has become my teacher and my path has become to help others who are just at the beginning of this journey.

The following three activities are intended to support individuals with chronic pain or other chronic health conditions with finding their inner superhero.

The Hero in You

Batgirl (real name Barbara Gordon) is one of the most incredible superheroes of the DC universe. She is a librarian by day and a superhero by night. When the Joker paralyzes her, Barbara Gordon can't use her legs to fight crime but she is able to adopt a new superhero persona—Oracle, who can use library science and research skills to help the Justice League fight the most notorious supervillains.

Harry Potter often experiences excruciating migraines, especially when he is in potential danger. But he manages to use this ability to help him.

Sometimes, due to an accident or a new health condition, we might not be able to do some of the things that we used to be able to do. For example, someone who was paralyzed after an accident might not be able to run but this does not mean that they are unable to play sports or spend time with their friends.

If your abilities changed as a result of an accident, a trauma, or a health issue (including mental health), what are some of the things that you find yourself missing? For example, you might miss being able to run, dance, or travel.

In the space below, please write out which activities or experiences you might be missing, something that you wish you were able to do.

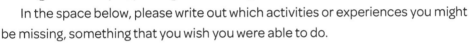

_____

_____

_____

_____

_____

_____

_____

Oftentimes, we might think of certain activities in "all-or-none" terms—"Either I can do it or I can't." For example, someone who used to play football might think that they are unable to play if their leg is broken or if they are unable to walk. As a result, they might stay away from everything related to football, including talking to friends about it, watching it on television, or finding other ways to participate.

It is true that with a change in our health condition there will be certain changes that will be out of our control. This means that things will not be the same as they used to be, possibly forever.

You have every right to grieve this loss. It hurts. It must be excruciating. And anyone in your situation would feel the same way.

There is a reason why you are feeling as much emotional pain as you are—it is because you care. Think about what makes you care. What are some of the most important aspects of this activity for you? For example, perhaps it allows you to spend time with friends, to exercise, gives you something to look forward to, and something to talk about with your family and friends.

Please write out some of these important aspects of this activity below.

_____

_____

_____

_____

_____

_____

_____

Now that you have identified the most important aspects of this activity, see if you can think about a few other ways that you can engage in these aspects, such as by spending time with your friends, attending practices even if you are not playing, encouraging others, finding ways to play within your level of ability (e.g., playing from a wheelchair).

It is true that these activities will not be the same as before you experienced a change in your condition. And yet, it seems so important to you that the fighter, the hero within you, would probably rather be a part of what is really important to you than not at all, just like Batgirl and like so many other heroes whose abilities had to be limited by an injury or illness.

Being able to show up while you are already managing your new condition is heroic and can be helpful not only to you. It can inspire others to do the same.

Channeling the inner hero within yourself, please identify ways in which you can still partake in activities that are important to you.

_____

_____

_____

_____

_____

_____

☆

Finding a Sense of Balance

Sometimes, when we go through a new pain or health (physical or mental health) condition, we might pull away from everything, afraid to trigger the painful experience, afraid to make it worse. Unfortunately, when we pull back on everything that gives us meaning, we are not fully protecting ourselves. Instead, we might be withdrawing from everything that gives us meaning. To some degree, it might make sense—if we push ourselves too far, we might get hurt again. However, sometimes we might go overboard with our safety behaviors, so much so that we might miss out on opportunities for connection, joy, and meaning. So, perhaps you might be able to find a balance in which you can still engage in meaningful activities without overdoing it or re-injuring yourself.

What might be some of the ways that you can find a sense of balance between doing what you care about while being aware of your health condition?

For example, Superman cares about saving people. So, he spends as much time as possible helping others. However, when he is overwhelmed, or after he is exposed to kryptonite, Superman needs to rest. He might take some time in the Fortress of Solitude until his exhaustion or his pain levels subside, and then he will return to helping people.

See if you can think of some ways in which, like Superman, you can find a sense of balance between doing something you care about and being mindful of taking care of your health.

_____

_____

_____

_____

_____

_____

_____

_____

_____

_____

_____

Your Inner Superhero

(AGES 7–10)

All heroes go through a hard time sometimes, including Batman, Wonder Woman, and Harry Potter. It's not easy to feel ill a lot of the time and facing your illness is your biggest superpower.

Let's try an exercise to help you find your own inner superhero. First, please draw (or write) some of the activities that you like to do with your friends and family (even if you can't do some of them now).

Great! Good job! These activities point out what you care about, such as spending time with your friends and family, playing, or watching films or TV shows.

Now, see if you can think of a few ways that you can still engage in some of these activities, at least a little bit. Feel free to draw or write your responses.

Well done. Now, imagine that you are a superhero. You can help other people and have any superpowers you would like. What kind of costume would you have? What kinds of superpowers would you have? How would you use these to help people? Please draw or write your ideas below.

Although trauma is not necessary for finding our sense of meaning, many people who have experienced a traumatic event report that their priorities and life trajectories have changed. In fact, many individuals who undergo a traumatic experience or another type of extreme adversity or challenge might develop posttraumatic growth (PTG; Pollard and Kennedy, 2007; Tedeschi and Calhoun, 1996). PTG refers to the experience of a positive change as a result of a struggle, resulting in improved interpersonal relationships, increased personal strength, changed priorities, and an improved sense of life appreciation and gratitude (Tedeschi and Calhoun, 1996).

The biggest contributor to posttraumatic growth is meaning making, which means finding a sense of purpose in our own experience (Park and Ai, 2006). Meaning making has been shown to help people reduce PTSD symptoms and be a predictor of overall wellbeing (Alea and Bluck, 2013; Park and Ai, 2006). Developing a sense of purpose can include accepting our physical and emotional pain as not only a part of our life, but also as our teacher (LeJeune and Luoma, 2019). In addition, a sense of purpose can also involve learning from our experiences and using it to help others. Finally, a sense of purpose can bring a clarification of our core values, which can subsequently guide our superhero steps (Scarlet, 2016).

The following two activities are designed to assist clients with accepting their pain as their teacher and with meaning making. For younger clients or those with developmental, learning, or physical disabilities, the therapist can fill out the answers in the spaces provided.

Pain Is My Teacher

(AGES 11 AND UP)

What do Batman, Harry Potter, and Wonder Woman have in common? They have all been through high levels of physical and emotional pain. They have all lost someone they loved. And they have all learned to help other people because of it.

Sometimes we find lessons in the most unexpected situations. Our painful experiences can sometimes teach us very important lessons. For example, if you burn your finger on a hot stove, you might learn not to touch hot surfaces. Similarly, if you lost someone you care about, such as a grandparent, a pet, or a friend, you might learn to treasure other people in your life.

Take a few moments to think about something painful that you have been through, which could be physical pain—such as a headache, a broken bone, or a burn—or emotional pain, such as sadness, fear, or grief.

What has this type of pain made you aware of? What has it taught you?

_____

_____

_____

Interestingly, sometimes our greatest fears and our deepest pain point to what we care about the most. For example, if you fear losing your friends, this would suggest that you care about your friendships. If you were heartbroken over a breakup, it would suggest that you value your relationship. Looking at it from this perspective, what are some of your painful experiences suggesting about what you care about?

_____

_____

_____

Learning more about your pain can allow you to also learn about what is important to you, as well as how to value and cherish experiences that are meaningful to you. For example, the death of a loved one can remind us of the importance of spending time with people who are still around and might remind us to refocus on what is actually important in our lives, instead of our to-do lists and busy schedules.

What are some aspects in your life that are very important to you that you would never want to take for granted, such as your family, your friends, your pet, your gaming or your favorite shows, or others?

_____

_____

_____

Meaning Making

Imagine for a moment that there is another person who is going through what you went through. But unlike you, this person is at the very beginning of their journey, meaning that this event, this struggle that you have been going through, has only now begun for them. Imagine if you could mentor this person, support them, or help them in some kind of way, not unlike how Batman supports other people who are struggling. You can learn from your pain and experiences to now become a mentor, a hero to help others.

What would you do or say to help this person? Please write out or draw your answer.

This is your purpose—one of many—you are here because you are destined to make a difference. Please know that you are important and your quest is only beginning. Where would you like to start?

Fanfiction

A unique vehicle for meaning making using popular culture is fanfiction (Vinney and Dill-Shackleford, 2018). Fanfiction refers to creating an original piece of fiction using existing copyrighted franchises, such as *Harry Potter*, *Justice League*, *Star Wars*, *Supernatural*, *Avengers*, and others. Fans of these particular franchises (i.e., fandoms) might rewrite certain scenes from pre-existing stories to make meaning of a particular event in the story, for example, to give the character more agency, to expand their story, or to include diverse perspectives (e.g., LGBTQ themes).

The Fanfic Vocabulary table contains fanfiction vocabulary for the therapist when engaging with clients who enjoy fanfiction.

Fanfic Vocabulary

Term	Definition
FanArt	Creating an original artwork within the existing fandom or characters (e.g., Batman with a lightsaber)
Fanfiction (fanfic)	Writing an original story within the existing fandom (e.g., Harry Potter)
Archive of Our Own (A03)	Popular fanfic publication website
Fandom	Popular culture franchise (e.g., Harry Potter fandom)
Con	Short for convention, such as comic convention
Expo	Short for exposition, similar to a convention but primarily focused on exhibits and demonstrations (e.g., of new video games)
Cosplay	Dressing up as fictional characters; can be a profession
Cosplayer	Someone who cosplays
Meme	Humorous image, text, or video that is widely shared on the internet
Fanboy/Fangirl	Someone who gets excited about something fan-related, such as a celebrity
Shipping	Ship is short for Relationship. Shipping characters refers to writing about (or wishing to see) two characters together as having a relationship
OTP	One True Pair—the characters someone wants to see in a relationship together more than any other characters
Slash fanfic	Same sex shipping in fanfic (writing about same sex characters as having a relationship)
Canon	Something that is factually established within the actual fandom (for example, Batman lives in Gotham City—this is canon)
Fanon	Something that is unofficial, established by fans
Crossover	Having fanfic characters from multiple fandom universes (e.g., Harry Potter fighting monsters with Batman)
Trolling	Online bullying/cyberbullying
POV	Point of view (for example, rewriting the book from another character's POV)
SI	Self-insertion—incorporating oneself into fanfic

The following two activities are two different variants that can be utilized to help clients to use fanfiction or FanArt to connect with their sense of purpose.

Fanfic Writing

Pick a scene from your favorite book, movie, TV show, or comic book that really upset you. Perhaps it was a scene that included a death of a character that you didn't want to see die or someone who was mistreated in some way.

Write this scene to the best of your memory in the space provided below. Write as many details as you can remember, such as what happened and what was said. It doesn't have to be 100 percent accurate. Don't focus on getting it "right"—just write it out.

_____

_____

_____

_____

_____

_____

_____

_____

_____

_____

_____

_____

_____

_____

Now see if you can write yourself into that scene and change the story in any way that you would like. Don't worry about making it "perfect"—just write it out.

_____

_____

_____

_____

_____

☆

_____

_____

_____

_____

_____

_____

_____

_____

What was it about this scene that upset you and what made you want to change it in this way?

_____

_____

_____

_____

_____

_____

_____

_____

_____

_____

_____

_____

_____

FanArt for Teens/Adults

Pick a scene from your favorite book, movie, TV show, or comic book that really upset you. Perhaps it was a scene that included the death of a character that you didn't want to see die or someone who was mistreated in some way.

Draw this scene to the best of your memory in the space provided below. Draw it out as a comic book—stick figures are perfectly fine. You can use thought bubbles and speech bubbles if you'd like. The scene doesn't have to be 100 percent accurate. Don't focus on getting it "right"—just draw it.

Now see if you can draw yourself into that scene and change the story in any way that you would like. Don't worry about making it "perfect."

What was it about this scene that upset you and what made you want to change it in this way?

FanArt for Kids

Please draw your favorite superhero or another favorite fictional character below. Don't worry about making it perfect—just draw this character the best way that you can.

Now, see if you can draw one or two pictures where you get to talk to this character. Maybe you get to support this character or maybe this character supports you in some way. Or maybe you help other people.

Now, draw yourself helping other people in your life as a kind of superhero.

The Fanfic Writing and FanArt exercises described above can be used to help the client to develop their own sense of purpose by demonstrating to them the kind of issues that affect them and how they would like to make a difference in these kinds of situations. These exercises can be further utilized to help the client identify their core values and to begin planning toward taking actions in accordance with those core values.

Cosplay

Similar to fanfiction, cosplay can also be used in therapy to help clients to discover their sense of purpose and prepare them for action. In fact, a finding by White and Carlson (2015) suggests that dressing up like their favorite characters can help children to maintain attention on a task, such as homework. Cosplay can represent a sense of a person's identity (Rosenberg and Letamendi, 2013) as well as their interests and values.

The activity that follows provides an example of how cosplay might be incorporated into therapy to help the client to consider their own sense of heroic purpose.

Cosplay Your Inner Hero

Do you ever cosplay (dress up like some of the characters you like)? Let's imagine that you could design your own hero costume that most represents who you are and what you stand for. Would you have a superhero cape, a magic wand with a witch/wizard robe, or another costume?

What would it look like? How might it empower you? How might it represent who you are? Please draw or write about your hero costume in as much detail as possible.

Great job! This costume might represent you, but the real hero is inside your heart and has always been there. Sometimes, it can help to wear something that can remind us of our inner abilities. Do you have anything that you could wear (maybe a small item, like a bracelet) to remind you of your heroic identity and your sense of purpose?

Core values

An important part of helping a client to establish their sense of purpose is to help them identify their core values. Core values (unlike goals) are infinite. Core values are valued life directions, whereas goals are finite steps toward honoring those core values (Hayes *et al.*, 2006). For example, helping people might be a core value, whereas helping a friend with math homework today might be a goal.

The following four activities are designed to help clients to discover their own core values as a part of their sense of purpose in order to get them ready to take steps to become their own version of a superhero in real life (IRL). For younger clients or those with developmental, learning, or physical disabilities, the therapist can fill out the answers in the provided spaces.

Three Superpowers

If anything were possible, and if you could be granted three superpowers or magical abilities, what would you wish for?

_____

_____

_____

_____

_____

_____

_____

What would make you want those powers?

_____

_____

_____

_____

_____

_____

_____

_____

What would you do with them?

_____

_____

_____

_____

_____

_____

_____

_____

Magic Crystal

Let's imagine for a moment that you meet a magical genie and this genie is able to give you exactly the life that you would want. And let's imagine that you can look into a magic crystal, just as Harry Potter looked into the Mirror of Erised, and see your life exactly as you would want it to be.

What would you see in this magic crystal? What would you be doing? Who would you be with? What would your life be like? Which parts of it would really make you happy?

The Vials of Meaning[1]

Our *core values* are our life directions, the qualities, beliefs, or principles that guide our lives. For Harry Potter, for example, some of his core values included family, friends, his pet owl, Hedwig, as well as standing up for those who can't stand up for themselves, standing up to evil, doing the right thing, and fighting for the truth.

Core values need to be distinguished from goals. Whereas core values are never-ending life directions, goals are finite (have an end). For example, one of Batman's core values is helping people, while one of his goals might be to stop the Joker from robbing a bank.

Our core values can be difficult to balance. Sometimes we put a lot of time and effort into some of them, while at other times we might neglect them altogether.

We can think of core values as potion vials. Sometimes, if we put too much time into them, the vials overflow. At other times the vials might be only half full or near empty. The illustration below shows several rows of core values vials, each represented as "empty." Take a look at these and consider where you currently are with your core values. In particular, take a look at how much time and effort you are currently putting into each of these core values based on where you'd like to be. You can then shade in the amount of potion that represents where you currently are in terms of meeting this core value.

As you are working on this exercise, keep in mind that the exact definitions of these core values are also up to your interpretation, no one else's. For instance, *family* could mean blood-related family, or it could mean chosen family, like we see in *Harry Potter, Supernatural,* or the *X-Men.*

Some values might also overlap. Creativity and fandom might both include cosplay or writing fanfiction.

For this exercise, identify your own definitions for each core value. Whatever these core values mean to you, the definitions for each are yours, and yours alone.

If you are perfectly happy with the amount of time and effort you are putting into your specific core value (such as *friends*), then you shade the bottle as full but not overflowing. If you think you are spending too much time on your career, for example, then that potion bottle would be overflowing. If you're not spending enough time on a particular core value, then your potion bottle would be less full, or even empty. Also, feel free to add your own vials to this if there are values that aren't represented. Give it a try now.

---

1   Adapted from Scarlet (2017).

  161

What Is Your Quest?

Let's imagine that 30 years from now, there is a movie about you. It is a superhero-like Hollywood movie. It tells your inspirational story about how much impact you've made in the lives of others and how much you've helped other people and important causes.

Take a moment to consider that you have already made a meaningful impact in the lives of others and consider how in the future, you, your work, or your legacy can continue to help other people. What would that movie ideally be about?

_____

_____

_____

_____

_____

_____

_____

_____

If this film did exactly what it is supposed to, how would you want it to inspire/ affect others? What kind of an inspiring message would you want the viewers to walk away with?

_____

_____

_____

_____

_____

_____

_____

_____

_____

☆

Remember this: Just as the client is on their own heroic quest, so are you on yours. Your actions inspire other people and your kindness is changing lives. On the days when you might feel burned out, exhausted, and unmotivated, remember that each step you take, each kind action that you make, they all make a difference.

Chapter 8

SUPERHERO IRL

I will never forget that day. I was having a horrific migraine, causing me to lose balance as I moved. My vision kept going in and out. I was on my eighth panic attack for the day and was on the way to be the keynote speaker for the Harry Potter Academic Conference in Los Angeles.

The excruciating pain, the anguish of anxiety, and the crippling self-doubt made me burst into tears, as I was sure that I was going to do a terrible job or collapse on the floor. I told my partner that I wanted to cancel but he talked me into going. When I walked into the hall where I was supposed to present, I was shaking from both pain and fear and started walking toward the event organizer to apologize and tell her that I was simply too sick to present.

As I was an hour early, the hall was still mostly empty, with the exception of me, my partner, the organizer, and a teenager who was sitting in one of the chairs. As I started walking toward the organizer, the teenager got up from her chair and walked up to me.

"Excuse me, are you Dr. Scarlet?" she asked me.

"Yes." I nodded, fairly certain that I was going to collapse any minute.

"I just wanted to tell you that my mom and I drove for two hours to get here. I am very excited about your talk. I struggle with severe depression and *Harry Potter* saved my life. I'm looking forward to learning more about psychology tools that I can use to help me."

I stood there and stared at her for a moment. I took a breath, slowly finding the ground under my feet, my vision stabilizing. I looked at her and in that moment I remembered why I was there, in that hall, planning to give the talk that I was invited to do. I remembered then that it was not about me, my ego, my anxiety, or my "Imposter Syndrome." It was about what I could offer, it was about the people in that audience who were struggling and came to this lecture to learn how they can get through some of the most excruciating moments of their lives through the lens of their favorite fandom. This realization snapped me back to reality and allowed me to stay.

The pain was still there, as was my anxiety, but something else was there too—my sense of purpose and the commitment to take action, an action that was not about me but about other people. And somehow, changing that perspective allowed me to stay and allowed me to give the talk that I was invited to give. What I kept thinking about was that if my talk helped just one person, then I would have done my job, and nothing else really mattered after that.

After we are able to assist our clients in finding their sense of purpose, the next step in Superhero Therapy training is to help them with determining the kind of steps they would need to take in order to become their own version of a superhero IRL. Helping our clients to focus on their sense of purpose can remind them about how much of a difference they can make in the lives of others, it can allow them to make meaning, and can allow them to be more willing to participate in "superhero actions," such as exposures, committed actions, behavioral activation techniques, and other skills (Park, Riley, and Snyder, 2012; Reid *et al.*, 2017). Briefly, exposures are any steps that clients take to face their fears or discomforts, such as their phobias, social anxiety, and so on. Willingness to face discomfort and commitment to change appear to be the biggest predictors of client engagement in exposure practice (Reid *et al.*, 2017). By tying the exposure-based exercises to the client's sense of purpose, by reminding the client what they stand for, we can essentially increase their sense of willingness to partake in these exercises.

In this chapter, we are going to look at a few exercises about how to assist a client with taking actions toward becoming their own version of a hero in real life by tying these steps with the client's own sense of purpose. Here is an activity to help the client understand the importance of not only finding their sense of purpose, but also taking active steps toward becoming their own version of a hero IRL, even if it means facing their greatest fears over time. The second version of this activity (for 7- to 10-year-olds) could be completed either as a discussion-only exercise for the youngest or as a written exercise for the older end of the age range.

Something Bigger than Me for Teens/Adults

Think about a real or fictional hero, like Batgirl, Harry Potter, or the Winchester Brothers from *Supernatural*, or another character that you like. Are there any times when a character you admire has felt sad, scared, or unsure of themselves?

For example, there was a time when Harry Potter's best friend, Ron, had to face his fear of spiders, in order to help their mutual friend, Hermione. Similarly, the Winchester Brothers, who fight supernatural forces, like ghosts and vampires, often don't know the kind of monster that they are dealing with before they rush in to save someone who needs their help.

What allows these characters to face their biggest obstacles and fears? It has to do with remembering what they are doing it for. Remembering what they stand for allows multiple heroes, including Batgirl, Harry Potter, and the Winchesters, to face some of their greatest challenges even if they are feeling unsure of themselves. In many cases, the heroes are willing to try something new even if they don't know if they are going to succeed because doing something is better than doing nothing.

Most people spend all their time and energy running away from what they *don't want*—painful emotions, memories, sensations. But life isn't about running away from what you don't want; it's about going after what you *do want*. It's about taking chances and following your heart. It's about falling down and getting up again. It's about not giving up in the face of challenges; it's about remembering what you stand for and showing up like the hero that you are.

So, let's take a look at some of the steps these heroes take in order to overcome some of the obstacles they are facing:

1. **Learning:** They try to learn as much about the monster or obstacle they are facing as possible to maximize their chances of overcoming it.
2. **Plan:** Heroes form a plan about how they will face a specific monster and often recruit sidekicks to help them. They also focus on the big picture—on what the mission is for.
3. **Attempt the plan:** Once the heroes form a plan, they try it out, even if they aren't sure if it will be successful, because they know that doing something is better than doing nothing.
4. **Learn from the results:** Heroes rarely ever fully succeed on the first try. Instead, every time they try to face their monsters, they learn something. With time, the heroes become less afraid of their monsters and learn ways to face them.
5. **Form new plans:** Using the information from the initial plan, the heroes can create new plans to face their monsters.
6. **Try again:** The more the heroes learn about the monsters they are facing, the better they can learn to face their monsters.
7. **Keep trying and never give up:** The most impressive heroes are ones who keep trying and never give up. They remember their mission as something greater than themselves. They might overcome some challenges and others might arise. The key is to never give up and to keep "superheroing."

What are some small steps I can take?

Think about a monster you frequently face. For this practice, don't start with the scariest monster you face. Pick a fairly manageable one (no more than 6/10 difficulty level) and see if you can practice with these steps:

1. Learning: What can you learn from this monster and what do you already know?

_____

_____

_____

2. Plan: Put together a plan for taking one small action to face this monster. Remind yourself what you're doing it for. What's the big picture? For example, it could be being able to spend more time with your friends.

_____

_____

_____

3. Attempt the plan: Try it out.

4. Learn from the results: Record your experience.

_____

_____

_____

5. Form new plans: Using the information from the initial plan, create new plans to face your monster.

_____

_____

_____

6. Try again.

7. Keep trying and never give up: Remember what it is all for. Remember that you are a superhero and that you facing your monsters is going to help other people.

Remember: It isn't about avoiding what you _don't_ want; it's about going after what you _do_ want. Focus on that, and the rest will come. Keep "superheroing."

Something Bigger than Me for Kids

Think about a real or fictional hero, like Batman, Spider-Man or Wonder Woman, for example. Most superheroes face some challenges and do not always succeed when they try to do something.

The truth is that many of us do not succeed at something at first, but the more we keep trying, the more chances we have to succeed in the end. If you ever play a game, for example, you might not win at first, but if you keep trying, you will eventually figure it out.

So, let's take a look at some of the steps these heroes take so they can overcome some of the obstacles they are facing:

1. **Learning:** They try to learn as much about the monster or obstacle they are facing as possible to give them the best chance of overcoming it.
2. **Plan:** Heroes make a plan about how they will face a specific monster and often get a sidekick to help them. They also focus on what the mission is for.
3. **Try out the plan:** Once the heroes make a plan, they try it out, even if they aren't sure if it will be successful. They try it out because they know that doing something is better than doing nothing.
4. **Learn from the results:** Heroes don't often succeed on the first try. Instead, every time they try to face their monsters, they learn something. With time, the heroes become less afraid of their monsters and learn ways to face them.
5. **Make new plans:** Using the information from the first plan, the heroes can create new plans to face their monsters.
6. **Try again:** The more the heroes learn about the monsters they are facing, the better they can learn to face their monsters.
7. **Keep trying and never give up:** The most impressive heroes are ones who keep trying and never give up. They think about their mission as something greater than themselves. They might overcome some challenges and others might arise. The key is to never give up and to keep "superheroing."

What are some small steps I can take?

Now, let's think about some challenges you might face and let's discuss some ways you can create a plan and take steps to succeed, just like your favorite superheroes do.

1. **Learning:** What do I already know about the challenge I am facing? (For example, it could be a homework problem or a conflict with someone in your family.)

_____

_____

_____

_____

2. **Plan:** Put together a plan for taking one small step to face this challenge.

_____

_____

_____

_____

_____

3. **Attempt the plan**: What might be the way to try it out?

4. **Learn from the results**:

_____

_____

_____

_____

_____

5. **Make new plans:** Using the information from your first plan, create new plans to face your challenge.

_____

_____

_____

_____

_____

6. **Try again.**

7. **Keep trying and never give up.**

SUPERHERO IRL   ☆   171

Many clients might be motivated to make changes but might become disappointed if they are not seeing results as quickly as they would like. Many might be comparing their starting point to where they want to end up as a way to shame themselves or demotivate themselves. I can relate to this personally. I used to think that I couldn't run. Between a knee injury and being out of shape and out of practice, I used to look at other people around me and be disappointed that I couldn't run more than a minute without feeling out of breath.

Then one day, I changed my goal. I decided that I would just run from one streetlight to the next one, a distance of about 95 feet. I was able to do that even though I ran slowly and felt out of breath by the time I got there. Then, my goal became to make it to the next one. After 2 months of very gradually increasing my distance, I was able to run 3 miles. It took 3 years for me to be able to run a marathon and what kept me going that entire time was just the motto, *Just make it to the next streetlight. That's all. Just make it to the next one.*

In order to help clients set realistic short-term goals, I have developed the following activity. There are two versions: one for older children, teens and adults, and one for younger children.

Climbing a Mountain for Teens/Adults

Wonder Woman is an amazing superhero and warrior. But she did not become a warrior overnight. Wonder Woman (birth name, Diana) has to practice her skills every day to become the warrior that she grows into. Similarly, Bruce Wayne trains for years to become Batman, and Harry Potter and his friends spend years studying magic before they are able to do it proficiently.

Oftentimes we set goals for ourselves that might seem like we have to climb a mountain to get there. When we are standing on the ground and looking up, the mountain might seem impossible to climb, so we might give up without even trying.

What might be a mountain you're trying to climb? For example, it could be running a marathon, finishing all your homework, or finishing your chores.

_____

_____

_____

_____

_____

_____

The way we can climb the mountain is by climbing one step at a time. Focus only on the next step. What is the next step you need to take to get you just a tiny bit closer to the top?

_____

_____

_____

_____

_____

Remember how much heroes practice every day to get to where they are. Imagine your favorite hero or character practicing, feeling frustrated at times, but continuing to practice. That's exactly what you are doing. Remember that this practice is exactly that—*practice*. And that means that sometimes you might take the wrong step, but that's okay! You are not starting over from the beginning. You just have to go back to a previous step and then try another one. What can you remind yourself of when you feel like giving up?

_____

_____

_____

_____

_____

_____

Visualize your success to remind you what you are fighting for. Imagine yourself succeeding. Imagine being able to climb that mountain—being able to run that marathon, being able to finish your work, your project, getting to your goal. What would that be like?

_____

_____

_____

_____

_____

_____

No matter what, don't ever give up on what is truly important to you. Try and try again. Don't wait for your life to be over to try it out. Start now. Take one small step up, just climb up a quarter of an inch and keep going!

Climbing a Mountain for Kids

Wonder Woman is an amazing superhero and warrior. Bruce Wayne trained for many years to become Batman, and Harry Potter and his friends spend many years studying magic before they are able to do it well.

Sometimes we have goals that seem like we have to climb a mountain to get there. For example, cleaning our room or doing homework might seem like an impossible goal when we have a lot of work to do.

See if you can draw a tall mountain and draw a tiny picture of yourself standing at the bottom of it. The mountain stands for the task that you need to complete. Looking at it this way, it might seem like climbing the mountain is impossible.

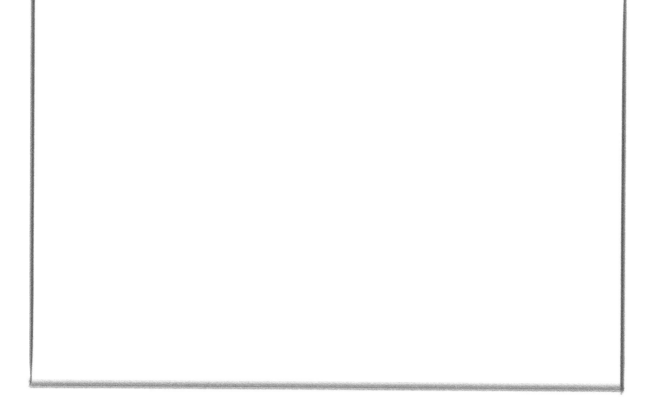

Now, draw steps that go up the mountain. All you have to do is to go up one step. And then another. And then another. Looking at your task this way can make it feel easier.

No matter what, don't ever give up on what is truly important to you. Try and try again. Take one small step up. Just climb up one step and keep going!

Finding inner motivation

It's neither a secret nor a surprise that clients who struggle with mental health issues might also struggle with finding the motivation to engage in certain therapy exercises, including ones that require them to face their fear or discomfort. One way to help individuals to increase their motivation and adherence to treatment is to help them increase their sense of self-efficacy, or the belief that they are capable of completing the task successfully (Margolis and McCabe, 2006). The following activity is intended to assist clients with increasing their sense of self-efficacy.

Letters to Batman

Imagine for a moment that you and Batman are the best of friends. And imagine that Batman is going through a hard time—he is struggling with the same thing as you. He has the same fears, anxieties, thoughts, and feelings as you, and he is thinking about giving up.

   Please write him an encouraging letter of support, speaking from your own experience, to help him get through it.

_____

_____

_____

_____

_____

_____

_____

_____

_____

_____

_____

_____

_____

_____

_____

_____

_____

_____

_____

_____

Small steps

Some folks may have an idea of their sense of purpose and how they would like to be a hero in their own way, but may believe that they don't make a difference or may not know where to start. The following two activities invite clients to consider small steps toward altruistic actions that can align with their sense of purpose.

Speaking Up and Showing Up

What does it mean to be a superhero in real life (IRL)? Well, to start, it means standing for something, it means remembering your sense of purpose, such as helping people, standing up for what you believe in, such as equality, peace, or justice. And it means taking small (or large) actions to speak up about what you believe in and show up to support this cause.

For example, Juanita, a 10-year-old girl in California, was being bullied. At first she thought she was alone in this experience but when she started paying attention to the bullying patterns, she realized that a number of other kids in her school were also being bullied. In order to stand up for the kids that were bullied, Juanita posted an encouraging note on the locker of all the kids in her school, spreading messages of care and kindness.

In another example, an 8-year-old boy, Ewan (now called Super Ewan), started a collection of food to make sandwiches for homeless individuals in his town. Since then, he's been able to start a non-profit helping many homeless individuals to have access to food, as well as warm clothes, all of which come from donations.

Both Ewan and Juanita started their journeys through small steps by speaking up about what they care about—helping others—whether through words or actions.

What's a small kind thing you can do or say to someone today that allows you to speak up or show up for what you believe in? Remember, the action doesn't have to be a big one, but it can make a big difference for someone else. For example, reaching out to someone who might be getting bullied and spending some time with them, or making one sandwich for someone who might not be able to afford it, could be a big step toward your journey of becoming a superhero IRL.

Write down one or two ideas of what you might be able to do today to speak up or show up.

_____

_____

_____

_____

It's okay if other people don't agree with you or don't share your views. Remember what it is for, remember the big picture, and remember that it all starts with small steps.

Superhero Steps for Teens/Adults

Have you ever wished that you could be a part of a fictional universe, like *Harry Potter, Supernatural,* or the DC Universe, for example? Have you ever wondered what you would do if you had certain superpowers or magical abilities? Have you thought what you might do if you could help other people?

Well, here is your chance. THIS IS THAT MOMENT. Your experiences and your abilities might be exactly what someone else really needs right now. For example, your kindness can be your superpower; your experience with your fears, your anxiety, or your painful events have brought you here, so that you can help others who are going through a hard time now too.

And now, YOU ARE THE CHOSEN ONE. This is *your* journey, *your* adventure, and *your* call to action. It has to be you. You are the only one who can do this.

What are some of the steps that you can take to be your very own version of a superhero? Write or draw your answer below.

Superhero Steps for Kids

(AGES 7 TO 12)

Have you ever wished that you could be a superhero or have magical powers like Harry Potter?

What kinds of superpowers or magical abilities do you wish you could have?

What would you do with those magical abilities or superpowers?

Now, imagine yourself having these superpowers. Draw yourself as a superhero doing powerful or heroic things, like facing your fears and helping your family and your friends.

The depth of resilience

Many clients may struggle to believe that they can make a difference in anyone else's life, often getting hung up on their surface level struggles, forgetting the numerous obstacles they have already overcome. To help clients understand the depth of their resilience, I like to use the Iceberg activity.

Iceberg

(AGES 11 AND UP)

In this image, we see an iceberg. To an outside observer, it seems like a small piece of ice in the middle of the ocean. But if we are able to see below the iceberg's surface, we see its might and depth.

Most of us are icebergs—with people around us only seeing a small portion of who we are, knowing a tiny amount of what we have been through and what we are capable of.

The tip of the iceberg represents your surface-level experiences and what some people might see. This might include your thoughts, your looks, or your external achievements or setbacks.

The depth of the iceberg represents what you have been through, such as your pain, your trauma, and what you have already survived as your resilience. It also represents what you stand for, such as your courage, your dedication to help others, or your commitment to good for this world.

Next to the tip of the iceberg, write down some words that people might see on the surface. Next to the depth of the iceberg, write down words that represent your strength, your struggles, your experiences, and your core values.

You are stronger than you might realize. Your roots run deeper than the surface level might allow you or anyone else to see at the moment. Remember how much you have already overcome. Remember the depth of you and your character. You are already a superhero. You have been since you were born, and your experiences have shaped you to be stronger than you might ever imagine.

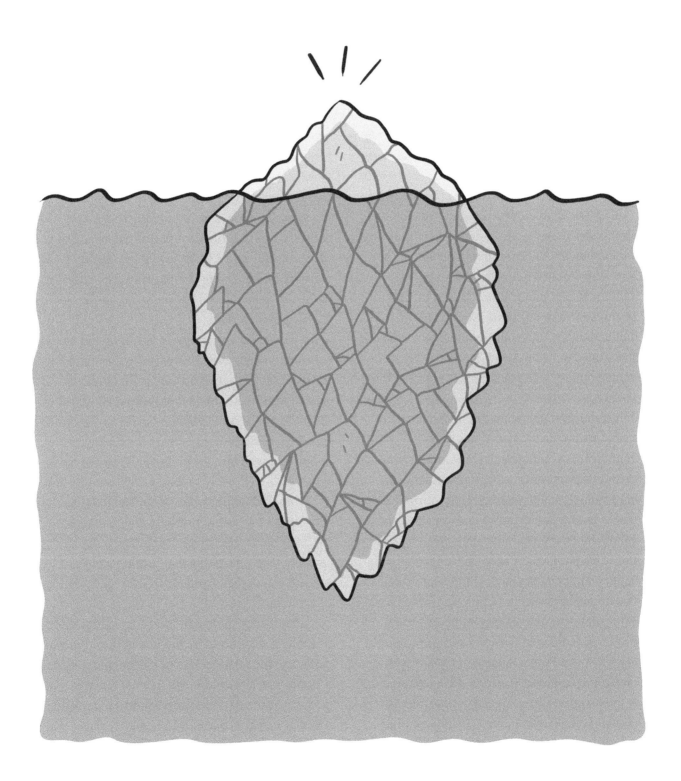

Some of our clients might be so fused with their anxiety that it might seem impossible for them to identify their sense of purpose, let alone the actions that they need to take to become a superhero IRL. However, sometimes, the client's anxiety itself can be utilized to help them discover their sense of purpose, allowing the therapist to help the client to formulate actions to become their own version of a hero.

For example, a few years ago I was working with a client with severe social anxiety. Let's call him "Clark." Clark was a manager at a big firm, and as such, frequently had to interview new employees, mentor staff, and give talks in front of large groups of people at his company.

Clark's origin story consisted of severe childhood abuse at the hands of his father, who shamed and beat him rather than encouraging him. His monsters consisted of crippling self-doubt and panic attacks when he had to be the centre of attention, such as before he had to deliver a speech. His monsters included thoughts like, "I am going to fail." "Everyone is judging me." "These speeches aren't helping anyone."

Clark's strategy for coping with these monsters was to avoid as many social interactions as possible. He would lock the door to his office, making himself unavailable to his employees. He would do everything in his power to avoid giving talks and training others.

When we started working together, Clark stated that one of his biggest heroes was Superman, because he could "defeat all odds and do the impossible." Clark also stated that Superman was able to inspire people to do good and to be good. When Clark completed the What Is a Personal Hero? exercise (see Chapter 4), he burst into tears. He revealed that in his imagined exercise, Superman sat next to him and encouraged him to believe in himself, to honor his obligations, and to take pride in his work. Clark said that in that moment the

imagined version of Superman was more of a father to him than his own father was.

Because of this exercise, Clark was able to identify his sense of purpose within his own anxiety. In analyzing his anxiety monsters, Clark realized that they were frightening him as a way of showing him what he really cared about—doing well at his job and helping others. In recognizing his sense of purpose, Clark's approach to his work-related responsibilities changed. He was still very anxious, but now he was viewing these anxieties as him rising to the challenge and charging up his superpowers, as well as accepting his heroic quest.

He started not only accepting presentation assignments but also requesting them. His anxiety was still high every time he would give his talks but now Clark viewed his anxiety as an important reminder of what was important to him and used it to be energetic and animated in his presentations.

The ultimate moment in his heroic journey occurred when after one of his presentations, one of Clark's mentees approached him and stated that he has always looked up to Clark. The mentee stated that he was always anxious about public speaking but seeing Clark give them inspired him and motivated him to try it out too.

In the following week when I asked Clark how it felt for him to not only give a speech *with his anxiety* (as opposed to *despite his anxiety*) and also to inspire another person, he smiled tearfully and said, "I felt like Superman."

Like "Clark," many of our clients might not initially realize that the inverse of their greatest fears are the foundations of our deepest sense of purpose. Hence, we can use the client's anxiety as a way to create a roadmap for the client's superhero steps. The activity that follows serves as an example of one way to approach this.

Superhero IRL

Sometimes our fears might hold us back from doing something important to us or following our goals. Instead of forcing the fears to go away, we can use them as information because the opposite of our fears is the map of what we care about the most.

This means that we can take a look at our fears and use them to learn how to take superhero actions. Here is how we can do that:

Step 1: Identify some of your biggest fears (for example, losing a loved one, being rejected or criticized, fear of making a mistake, fear of getting sick or dying). Write down some of your biggest fears below (or state them out loud).

_____

_____

_____

Step 2: Turn your fears around as an indicator of what you care about. For example, if you fear getting rejected, it might mean that you care about connection, belonging, and acceptance. If you fear losing a loved one, it might mean that this loved one is very important to you and you care about spending time with them. If you fear getting sick or dying, it might be because there are still many things you wish to do in this life.

Take some time to turn your fears into indications of what you care about.

_____

_____

_____

Step 3: Identify small steps you can take to participate in activities that you care about. For example, if you realized that you care about acceptance and connection, it might mean spending some time with people you want to remain connected to. Write down a few ideas of superhero actions you can take to honor what you care about the most.

_____

_____

_____

"Gamifying" mental health practices

For clients with anxiety disorders, such as social anxiety, panic disorder, agoraphobia, and other phobias who frequently avoid facing their fears, the following exercise about conquering their fear as a heroic game quest can be helpful. For more information about "gamifying" mental health practices and the usefulness of games in mental health, please check out Jane McGonigal's (2015) book: *SuperBetter: A Revolutionary Approach to Getting Stronger, Happier, Braver, and More Resilient.*

Gamify

(AGES 11 AND UP)

Every hero has to face their fears sometimes. For example, Batman used to be very afraid of bats. That was why he adopted a bat as his symbol, in order to conquer his fear. Harry Potter, and Dean Winchester from *Supernatural*, also have to face their fears on occasion.

Whether you fear sleeping alone, driving, flying on an airplane, being around people, or being in certain situations, these fears are your call to your quest to your being a real-life superhero and conquering your fears. Conquering your fears does not mean that you will not fear this situation any longer. It means that this fear no longer has to hold you back or stop you from what you want to or need to do.

In order to make facing your anxiety fun, we are going to treat it like a game, in which you get to level up every time you complete the requirements of a specific level. You also should assign little prizes to completing each level and a grand prize for completing the last level. You can always add more levels if you need to and you can face multiple fears at the same time or play them one at a time. You can also change the specific requirement of completing each level as you see fit.

Level 1: Facing this fear in your imagination. To complete this level, you need to write out (or talk about) facing this fear as if it was actually happening. You need to do it at least five times to complete this level.

Keep track of your completion of this game activity here.

_____

_____

_____

_____

_____

Write down the prize that you will get for completing this level.

_____

_____

_____

_____

_____

Copyright © Janina Scarlet—Superhero Therapy for Anxiety and Trauma—2021 ☆ 187

Level 2: Approach your feared situation but stay at a distance. For example, if you are scared of dogs, approach a dog but stay at least 20 feet away from it. If you are scared of flying, drive to the airport but don't get out of the car. Just hang out at the airport parking lot. You will be asked to do this a total of three times to complete this level.

Write out the specifics of completing this level and keep track of it here.

_____

_____

_____

_____

Write down the prize that you will get for completing this level.

_____

_____

_____

_____

Level 3: Engage in the feared activity for 30 seconds on five different occasions (if that is possible). For example, if you are scared of dogs, pet a dog for 30 seconds, or stand next to a dog for 30 seconds, on five different occasions.

Write out the specifics of completing this level and keep track of it here.

_____

_____

_____

_____

Write down the prize that you will get for completing this level.

_____

_____

_____

_____

☆

Level 4: Engage in the feared activity for 5 minutes on five different occasions (if that is possible). For example, if you are scared of dogs, stand next to a dog for 5 minutes. If you are scared of being in social situations, attend a social situation for 5 minutes on five different occasions.

Write out the specifics of completing this level and keep track of it here.

_____

_____

_____

_____

Write down the prize that you will get for completing this level.

_____

_____

_____

Level 5: Engage in the feared activity for 30 minutes on five different occasions (if that is possible). For example, if you are scared of dogs, stand next to a dog for 30 minutes. If you are scared of being in social situations, attend a social situation for 5 minutes on five different occasions.

Write out the specifics of completing this level and keep track of it here.

_____

_____

_____

_____

Write down the prize that you will get for completing this level and winning the game.

_____

_____

_____

_____

Each step you take to assist your client with becoming a hero of their journey can inspire them to believe in themselves in a way that they might not have realized was possible. Each client you meet is forever changed by you, by something you did or said to them. Even clients who had to drop out or be referred out, even clients who only saw you for one or two appointments are likely to still think of you because you listened, because you cared. You have already paved more of a way for your clients than you might ever realize. Thank you for caring. Thank you for changing lives on a daily basis.

Chapter 9

SURVIVOR STORY

We conducted the first session on either side of his bathroom door. "John" struggled not only with PTSD but also with severe agoraphobia and in the very first session we had together, he was too overwhelmed to come out of his bathroom. He apologized profusely on the other side of the door, crying and shaming himself. For the subsequent session, John was able to meet with me in his living room where it took him several sessions to find the courage to share his origin story with me—he witnessed a triple homicide which emotionally paralyzed him, preventing him from being able to go outside of his house and spending time with his friends and family. John believed that he was "incapable" of going outside and that if he did, he would "not be able to handle it."

John stated that he was a big fan of the British TV show about an alien Doctor—Doctor Who—who traveled through time and space to save people. John stated that he used to do missionary work as a child with his family and wished that he could go back to traveling to other countries to help people. Being able to help others became John's sense of purpose, allowing him to find the courage to face his fears and process his trauma.

I will never forget the moment that John and I stepped outside of his house together. He held my hand with one of his, and was holding onto the wall of his house with his other hand. He was shaking, he was crying. He

didn't think he would be able to do it, but there he was—standing outside of his house. After 20 minutes or so, John was able to let go of my hand and the house wall and stand on his own. By the end of the session, he was smiling and no longer shaking.

A few months later, he drove to my office and we were able to continue our sessions at the office. A few months after that, John completed his treatment, stating that he was leaving the country on a mission to help people in third world countries. By this time, his origin story narrative had changed to that of a survivor story.

A survivor story is the client's narrative from a survivor's perspective, which indicates what they faced, what they were able to overcome, as well as their resilience and sense of purpose. Here is a sample of John's survivor story:

"After witnessing [the triple homicide], I felt paralyzed with anxiety and was unable to leave the house for years. I missed school events and birthday parties. I thought I was keeping myself safe by staying in my house, but I felt more scared in running away from my trauma than when I was able to finally face it.

Facing my trauma made me realize that I am a survivor. I can be scared but I don't have to keep hiding in my house any more.

I am making a choice to face my anxiety and my past, my present, and my future. I choose to live my life by following my heart and helping other people in other countries, and in this work, I find my strength."

In rewriting their origin story, clients are likely to reduce their overall trauma and anxiety symptoms and also might have an easier time explaining their trauma to a family member or another ally (Deblinger *et al.*, 2011). The following activity can be used in helping clients to work on creating their survivor story narrative.

Rewriting Your Origin Story

(AGES 11 AND UP)

You are here. You have arrived at this moment—the time to turn your story into your survivor story. Everything you've experienced and have been through has led you to this moment.

I would like to invite you to think about yourself as a superhero, as a survivor, looking back to see how far you've come, and everything you've learned and overcome. You can also mention what you might have realized or learned as a result of this experience, as well as your sense of purpose.

If you are willing, please write out or draw your survivor story. If you wish, you can turn it into a comic book, an art piece, or a full-size book.

  193

Some clients might require more than one session to process their survivor story and may need to engage in this exercise every once in a while as a reminder of their resilience and self-efficacy. At the same time, some clients might struggle with shame about their current symptoms or past experiences. The following two activities are designed to reduce clients' experiences with shame as they are transitioning to their survivor journey.

Phoenix Reborn

Have you ever heard of a phoenix? A phoenix is a magical bird, said to come from the sun, that goes through painful changes every once in a while. After the phoenix has gone through a painful change, it bursts into burning flames and then falls to ash. But then the phoenix rises again, stronger than before.

In fact, sometimes our experiences, whether they are trauma, anxiety, or heartbreak, might feel like we are on fire. But like a phoenix, we might then rise from the ashes, stronger than before.

In the space below, please either draw or write a narrative (story) portraying yourself as a phoenix rising from the ashes.

Boxes and Unicorns

Sometimes what you want and what others want you to be are different, and that's okay. The truth is that we are not meant to be cookie-cutter clones of other people. This means that just because someone else has outlined a path for us, whether it has to do with our career, choices of our school major, our hobbies, or choosing our friends or partners, we have the ability to make our own choices.

Some people might expect you to fit into a box of their expectations. But what if you are actually a unicorn? Unicorns don't belong in boxes. They live on rainbows and make their own choices. This means that you have the right to be you, to like what you like, and to make your own choices. In the space below, please either draw or write a narrative (story) portraying yourself as a unicorn stepping out of a box.

As mentioned in the previous chapters, meaning making has been found to be extremely helpful at assisting people with reducing their trauma and anxiety symptoms, as well as overall subjective wellbeing (Alea and Bluck, 2013; Park and Ai, 2006). One way to assist clients with meaning making is through encouraging them to become an advocate for others who are going through the same kinds of experiences as the client previously endured, thus putting the client in a mentor/guardian role and allowing them to make meaning from their painful experiences. The following activity was designed to assist clients with meaning making to become an advocate for others.

Being an Advocate

Like the true superhero that you are, you have been through a lot and have also overcome a lot. There are many people who might be just at the very beginning of their own heroic journey, people who could use an ally just like you.

As a part of you being a superhero IRL, what are some ways you might want to help other people who are going through what you went through, such as bullying, a loss, anxiety, trauma, or another experience? For example, you might want to send them a kind note of encouragement, or you might want to let them know that you have been through something similar. Or perhaps you can join or start a cause that helps people who have been through similar experiences. This is your call to be your own version of Batman, or another superhero, in real life.

Please list a few steps that you might like to take to help others who are going through similar situations and experiences as you went through. You can write or draw your answer below.

A few years ago, I was working with a 15-year-old client. Let's call her "Lisa." Lisa struggled with anxiety and depression and went through a lot of bullying in school. Lisa believed that no one cared about her and that everyone hated her.

Lisa struggled with discussing her mental health, often asking her parents to speak for her. She struggled with disclosing her mental health experiences, seemingly ashamed of them. However, she was willing to talk about her favorite TV show, *Veronica Mars*. She stated that she felt a strong sense of connection with the leading character and identified with her. As you might recall from previous chapters, identification with strong protagonists can empower clients to increase their own self-efficacy (Isberner *et al.*, 2019).

Having never previously heard of *Veronica Mars*, I decided to go home and watch the first episode of the show. I accidentally ended up watching the entire first season. In one night.

The show is psychologically rich and very powerful in terms of portraying a variety of issues that teenagers might face. As for the leading character, Veronica Mars, she experiences just about every kind of trauma that a teenager can go through—she gets drugged and assaulted at a party, her best friend is murdered, her parents are separated, her mother is addicted to substances, her boyfriend breaks up with her, and everyone in school hates her. And all of that occurs before the show even opens and the rest of the show has to do with Veronica learning to pick up the pieces.

What is exceptionally powerful, however, is the way Veronica copes with her trauma—she becomes a teen detective, almost a teenage version of Sherlock Holmes, and uses her detective skills to help people. This is a very powerful example of the protagonist displaying posttraumatic growth.

When I returned to see my client the following week, I informed her that I understood why she was so drawn to this show. We discussed what she liked about it and how she often felt like Veronica did when the show first opened—traumatized, depressed, and alone.

When I asked her if anyone else in school might have been struggling with mental health, Lisa said, "I don't know. Maybe one or two people."

I then asked her, "What would Veronica do?"

She looked up at me. She thought about it. And then she said, "Veronica wouldn't keep silent. She would do something... She'd make a speech."

I stood there, stunned. My client had never before volunteered to talk about her mental health to me or anyone else, let alone make a speech.

I asked her, "So, is this what you want to do?"

She said, "Yes."

We spent 2 weeks rehearsing and practicing. And then she did it. She stood in front of her class and delivered a 5-minute speech. She spoke about her mental health struggles and her experiences with bullying, and her feeling alone. She disclosed that there were times when she thought about suicide but also shared that she was in therapy and was starting to feel better. She invited people to talk to her at any time if they were either struggling or had any questions about their mental health.

The results of this were unlike what either of us anticipated. At the end of her speech, her classmates rushed to her, hugging her and thanking her for speaking out. Everyone was crying, including the teacher. By the end of the week, everyone in school found out about her speech. People were messaging her and stopping her in the hallway, sharing their stories and thanking her. After a few months, she started a mental health peer support group in her school. And although there are still times that Lisa struggles with her monsters, she now doesn't have to struggle alone.

Like Lisa, like Batman, like Veronica Mars, chances are that you too have faced numerous monsters in your life, and probably continue to face many of them still. And yet, like these heroes, you are both a hero and an ally to those who need your help the most. Even when it's hard, even when you might be feeling overwhelmed, you still show up for not only your patients, but for so many people in your life. And that is the true definition of a hero. Thank you for all your hard work. Thank you for making a difference.

Chapter 10

PREPARING FOR FUTURE OBSTACLES

Even after the conclusion of the most successful treatment, where the client might have met all of their goals and appear to be in full remission, they might still need some "take home" practice in order to maintain the progress that they have made. For this reason, in addition to reviewing the client's progress prior to their termination of therapy, it is also helpful to arm the client with practice tools, including learning to identify signs of a potential resurgence of past symptoms and a plan for how to meet these challenges. The following activities are designed to assist clients in identifying issues as they arise and as a plan for relapse prevention.

Emotional Safety Plan

The truth is that nearly every character that we love and care about—including T-Challa and Shuri (*Black Panther*), Alex Danvers (*Supergirl*), Diana (*Wonder Woman*), Frodo (*The Lord of the Rings*), Sam and Dean Winchester (*Supernatural*)—has a heavy burden they carry and invisible scars that no one else can see. For Frodo, who is carrying the cursed ring, sometimes taking a few steps toward his destination to Mordor is excruciating, not to mention exhausting.

Depression can feel that way sometimes, as can grief and trauma.

When times are challenging, it might be easy to forget the skills that we have learned and the allies that we have made along the way. That's why we are going to create an emotional safety plan for how to approach old problems and new obstacles when they arise.

First, please list or draw some of the previous challenges you've struggled with whether or not you continue to experience them today, for example, depression, anxiety, and other concerns.

```



```

Next, please write out or draw some of the symptoms that you might need to look out for, some signs that you might be facing these monsters again. For example, you might notice that you are feeling irritable, or not wanting to be around people, have a stomach ache or headache, or are feeling more sad or anxious than usual.

Finally, let's think about which skills you can use to help you support yourself and find a sense of emotional safety if you are faced with these obstacles again. For example, you might wish to go into your Batcave for some time or have an imaginary (or real) conversation with your mentor. Please write out or draw some examples of skills you can readily use if these problems were to arise again.

Daily Intention Setting

(AGES 11 AND UP)

Having goals can help us to focus on what we would like to work on, what we would like to accomplish. However, sometimes our goals can be vague and long term, such as finishing school or completing a project.

In order to stay on top of our goals and to be able to continue to work on being a superhero IRL, it is helpful to set a daily intention. A daily intention-setting practice is the commitment to a small action or a way of being that you would like to focus on that day.

For example, you can set an intention to focus on being more patient with others on a given day. You write down your intention and commit to practicing being more patient throughout the day. At the end of the day, you can check in with yourself to see how your practice went. This check in is never meant to be a shaming experience. Instead, the check in is to see what went well and which obstacles arose for you that day (for example, a fight with your best friend that you could not possibly foresee).

You can then reset your intention the next day (whether it would be the same or a different intention from the day before) and continue to practice. As a friendly reminder, the key about an intention-setting practice is that it is in fact a *practice,* which means that it is not meant to be perfect and there is no way of getting it wrong. The idea is just to try it out.

Let's try this exercise. First write down your intention for the day. Examples of daily intentions could include being more patient, being mindful, being kind, reaching out to friends, doing some work toward completing a project, spending some time cleaning, taking a few actions toward social justice, etc.

Please write down your intention for today.

_____

_____

_____

_____

_____

_____

_____

_____

_____

At the end of the day, please write out how this practice went. Please refrain from shaming yourself if you were unable to complete your daily intention. It is common and can happen to anyone. The key is to acknowledge a setback when it happens and to continue working toward your intended goal. Write out what went well and any obstacles that came up for you, as well as how you might want to manage these obstacles should they arise again.

_____

_____

_____

_____

_____

_____

_____

_____

_____

_____

_____

_____

_____

_____

_____

Continue this practice the next day and whenever possible.

Upon completing therapy, some clients might erroneously believe that they should never have to experience additional setbacks and that their symptoms should be gone forever. Some might therefore shame themselves for the inevitable setbacks that they might have, as all human beings have, and for the return of their symptoms. Many fear that if they experience anxiety, depression, or other previous symptoms again, it means that they have lost all of the progress they have gained in therapy and are "back to square one." Helping clients to understand that setbacks are common and do not necessarily mean that they have relapsed can enable clients to better manage their symptoms and better assist themselves when they are struggling. The following exercise was designed to help clients to identify setbacks and find ways to help themselves when setbacks arise.

Facing Setbacks

Everyone faces setbacks from time to time. A setback refers to an interruption of someone's progress. For example, when Wonder Woman plans to help innocent civilians during the First World War, she might experience a setback when one of her plans doesn't go as she might have hoped.

Although all heroes face obstacles, it does not mean that all hope is lost. Instead, it might mean that the hero will need to use some of their skills (such as a magic lasso, magical skills, Spidey senses, or other abilities) and possibly ask their fellow heroes for support as well.

Even after you have completed your therapy superhero training, there will be times when your old monsters might show up again and new ones might arise. Remember: a return of the old problems does not mean that you are back "at square one." In fact, you can't be because you have changed. You have learned many skills and as a result, you are not the same person you used to be. For example, Harry Potter might encounter a complicated spell or potion that he has not experienced before or he might face a return of his old symptoms (headaches or painful memories) but it does not mean that he has unlearned magic. He can still use the spells and tools he has at his disposal and ask his friends and mentors for help too.

In order to help you during those unpredictable setbacks, let's list out all the skills you have learned, especially the ones you have found to be helpful during your therapy/superhero training. You can write them out or draw them below.

My Emergency Skills List

Now that you've identified your emergency skills, let's also identify the big picture. For example, Batman's sense of purpose is helping people and making Gotham City safer for everyone. What is your sense of purpose? What is it all for? Please write out or draw your answer below.

Finally, please write out your inner strengths. Oftentimes we might forget how resilient we actually are, how kind we are, and how much we have already overcome. Please write or draw your greatest strengths below and write out one or two sentences of encouragement for yourself, such as "I believe in you," "You matter," or "You make a difference."

Maintenance practices

With every new skill, whether this is athletic or mental health related, it is important for the individual to continue to practice the skill after they have completed their training in order to maintain mastery. Although most clients might understand the importance of continued practice of the learned skills, some lose motivation or focus upon the completion of therapy, usually due to the loss of accountability. The following activity is designed to assist clients with maintenance of their acquired skills by turning practice into a game.

Gamify Your Progress

Congratulations! You are now graduating from your therapy program! Well done! All your hard work has led you here, to this day.

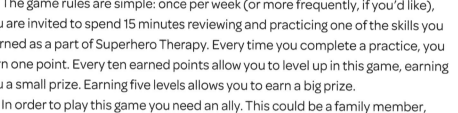

And much like any other skills, athletic or magical, it would be helpful to practice the skills you learned here. One fun way you can practice your Superhero Therapy training skills is by making them into a game.

The game rules are simple: once per week (or more frequently, if you'd like), you are invited to spend 15 minutes reviewing and practicing one of the skills you learned as a part of Superhero Therapy. Every time you complete a practice, you earn one point. Every ten earned points allow you to level up in this game, earning you a small prize. Earning five levels allows you to earn a big prize.

In order to play this game you need an ally. This could be a family member, a partner, or a friend who can help you to remember to practice and to decide which prizes you get for completing your levels.

Write out the name of your ally.

_____

_____

_____

_____

Write out an idea for a small prize you'd like to earn for completing ten points.

_____

_____

_____

_____

Write out an idea for a large prize you'd like to earn for completing five levels.

_____

_____

_____

_____

As you and your ally play the game, you can use the table below to keep track of your points.

Date	Skill(s) completed	Point(s) earned	Current level	Prize after completing this level	Prize after completing five levels
Level up!		Great job!	Keep going!		

Keep your eye on the prize and keep going! You are a superhero. Don't forget your cape.

Although your work with your client might end after their last session, your impact on their lives will continue well beyond it. You might not always remember every client you have ever worked with, but they will remember you. And during their most challenging times, they will think of you and might even have an imaginary counseling session with you.

Your work is extremely important, especially now. During a time of so much political unrest, the constant retraumatization from ongoing injustices, and global uncertainty and discourse, you play the most crucial role—supporting your clients in the fight for their lives. It is not easy to balance your clients' wellbeing and also to manage what you probably face on a daily basis as well. And just like Batman, you rise up every single day to save the world in your domain. Just like Wonder Woman, you don't let anyone set barriers between you and how many people you can help. Just like Harry Potter, your care and dedication are what make you truly magical even though you might not feel it or acknowledge it.

Taking on new work is not easy. Should you ever struggle, don't wait; reach out to your colleagues. Consult. Build your own Superhero league. Remember, you have already helped more people than you know. Someone is alive today because of something kind that you did or said and they might never think to tell you just how much your compassion has meant to them.

So, please always remember that you matter. Remember that your work matters and your work isn't done yet. Please keep "superheroing" and don't forget your cape.

References

Ahola, K., Väänänen, A., Koskinen, A., Kouvonen, A., and Shirom, A. (2010). Burnout as a predictor of all-cause mortality among industrial employees: a 10-year prospective register-linkage study. *Journal of Psychosomatic Research, 69*(1), 51–57.

Alea, N. and Bluck, S. (2013). When does meaning making predict subjective well-being? Examining young and older adults in two cultures. *Memory, 21*(1), 44–63.

Beaumont, E., Durkin, M., Hollins Martin, C.J., and Carson, J. (2016). Measuring relationships between self-compassion, compassion fatigue, burnout and well-being in student counsellors and student cognitive behavioural psychotherapists: a quantitative survey. *Counselling and Psychotherapy Research, 16*(1), 15–23.

Bellosta-Batalla, M., Blanco-Gandía, M.C., Rodríguez-Arias, M., Cebolla, A., Pérez-Blasco, J., and Moya-Albiol, L. (2020). Increased salivary oxytocin and empathy in students of clinical and health psychology after a mindfulness and compassion-based intervention. *Mindfulness, 11*(4), 1006–1017.

Bluth, K. and Neff, K.D. (2018). New frontiers in understanding the benefits of self-compassion. *Self and Identity, 17*(6), 605–608.

Bormann, J.E., Hurst, S., and Kelly, A. (2013). Responses to Mantram Repetition Program from veterans with posttraumatic stress disorder: a qualitative analysis. *Journal of Rehabilitation Research & Development, 50*(6), 769–784.

Brown, B. (2015). *Daring Greatly: How the Courage to Be Vulnerable Transforms the Way We Live, Love, Parent, and Lead.* New York: Penguin.

Cacioppo, J.T., Fowler, J.H., and Christakis, N.A. (2009). Alone in the crowd: the structure and spread of loneliness in a large social network. *Journal of Personality and Social Psychology, 97*(6), 977.

Carlson, L.E., Beattie, T.L., Giese-Davis, J., Faris, P. *et al.* (2015). Mindfulness-based cancer recovery and supportive-expressive therapy maintain telomere length relative to controls in distressed breast cancer survivors. *Cancer, 121*(3), 476–484.

Crespi, B.J. (2016). Oxytocin, testosterone, and human social cognition. *Biological Reviews, 91*(2), 390–408.

Cuddy, A.J., Wilmuth, C.A., and Carney, D.R. (2012). The benefit of power posing before a high-stakes social evaluation. *Harvard Business School Working Paper, No. 13-027.* Accessed on 8/02/2021 at http://nrs.harvard.edu/urn-3:HUL.InstRepos:9547823

Daigneault, I., Dion, J., Hébert, M., and Bourgeois, C. (2016). Mindfulness as mediator and moderator of post-traumatic symptomatology in adolescence following childhood sexual abuse or assault. *Mindfulness, 7*(6), 1306–1315.

Davidson, R.J., Kabat-Zinn, J., Schumacher, J., Rosenkranz, M. *et al.* (2003). Alterations in brain and immune function produced by mindfulness meditation. *Psychosomatic Medicine, 65*(4), 564–570.

Deblinger, E., Mannarino, A.P., Cohen, J.A., Runyon, M.K., and Steer, R.A. (2011). Trauma-focused cognitive behavioural therapy for children: impact of the trauma narrative and treatment length. *Depression and Anxiety, 28*(1), 67–75.

deRoon-Cassini, T.A., de St Aubin, E., Valvano, A.K., Hastings, J., and Brasel, K.J. (2013). Meaning-making appraisals relevant to adjustment for veterans with spinal cord injury. *Psychological Services, 10*(2), 186–193.

Derrick, J.E., Gabriel, S., and Hugenberg, K. (2009). Social surrogacy: how favored television programs provide the experience of belonging. *Journal of Experimental Social Psychology, 45*, 352–362.

Dezutter, J., Luyckx, K., and Wachholtz, A. (2015). Meaning in life in chronic pain patients over time: associations with pain experience and psychological well-being. *Journal of Behavioral Medicine, 38*(2), 384–396.

Dill-Shackleford, K.E., Vinney, C., and Hopper-Losenicky, K. (2016). Connecting the dots between fantasy and reality: the social psychology of our engagement with fictional narrative and its functional value. *Social and Personality Psychology Compass, 10*(11), 634–646.

Eisma, M.C., Stroebe, M.S., Schut, H.A., Stroebe, W., Boelen, P.A., and van den Bout, J. (2013). Avoidance processes mediate the relationship between rumination and symptoms of complicated grief and depression following loss. *Journal of Abnormal Psychology, 122*(4), 961–970.

Epel, E., Daubenmier, J., Moskowitz, J.T., Folkman, S., and Blackburn, E. (2009). Can meditation slow rate of cellular aging? Cognitive stress, mindfulness, and telomeres. *Annals of the New York Academy of Sciences, 1172*, 34.

Epel, E.S. and Lithgow, G.J. (2014). Stress biology and aging mechanisms: toward understanding the deep connection between adaptation to stress and longevity. *Journals of Gerontology Series A: Biomedical Sciences and Medical Sciences, 69*(Suppl_1), S10–S16.

Ford, T.E., Lappi, S.K., O'Connor, E.C., and Banos, N.C. (2017). Manipulating humor styles: engaging in self-enhancing humor reduces state anxiety. *Humor, 30*(2), 169–191.

Friedmann, E., Thomas, S.A., Liu, F., Morton PG *et al.* (2006). Relationship of depression, anxiety, and social isolation to chronic heart failure outpatient mortality. *American Heart Journal, 152*(5), 940–e1.

Gabriel, S., Read, J.P., Young, A.F., Bachrach, R.L., and Troisi, J.D. (2017). Social surrogate use in those exposed to trauma: I get by with a little help from my (fictional) friends. *Journal of Social and Clinical Psychology, 36*(1), 41–63.

Garbarino, J. (1987). Children's response to a sexual abuse prevention program: a study of the Spiderman comic. *Child Abuse and Neglect, 11*(1), 143–148.

Gilbert, P. (2010). An introduction to compassion focused therapy in cognitive behavior therapy. *International Journal of Cognitive Therapy, 3*(2), 97–112.

Granic, I., Lobel, A., and Engels, R.C. (2014). The benefits of playing video games. *American Psychologist, 69*(1), 66.

Hayes, S.C. (2019). *A Liberated Mind: How to Pivot Toward What Matters.* New York: Avery.

Hayes, S.C., Luoma, J.B., Bond, F.W., Masuda, A., and Lillis, J. (2006). Acceptance and commitment therapy: model, processes and outcomes. *Behaviour Research and Therapy, 44*(1), 1–25.

Heaney, J.L., Phillips, A.C., and Carroll, D. (2010). Ageing, depression, anxiety, social support and the diurnal rhythm and awakening response of salivary cortisol. *International Journal of Psychophysiology, 78*(3), 201–208.

Hoffman, Y.S., Pitcho-Prelorentzos, S., Ring, L., and Ben-Ezra, M. (2019). "Spidey Can": preliminary evidence showing arachnophobia symptom reduction due to superhero movie exposure. *Frontiers in Psychiatry, 10,* doi: 10.3389/fpsyt.2019.00354

Holmes, E.A., James, E.L., Coode-Bate, T., and Deeprose, C. (2009). Can playing the computer game "Tetris" reduce the build-up of flashbacks for trauma? A proposal from cognitive science. *PloS One, 4*(1), e4153.

Hucklebridge, F., Clow, A., and Evans, P. (1998). The relationship between salivary secretory immunoglobulin A and cortisol: neuroendocrine response to awakening and the diurnal cycle. *International Journal of Psychophysiology, 31*(1), 69–76.

Isberner, M.B., Richter, T., Schreiner, C., Eisenbach, Y., Sommer, C., and Appel, M. (2019). Empowering stories: transportation into narratives with strong protagonists increases self-related control beliefs. *Discourse Processes, 56*(8), 575–598.

Killingsworth, M.A. and Gilbert, D.T. (2010). A wandering mind is an unhappy mind. *Science, 330*(6006), 932.

Kiken, L.G., Lundberg, K.B., and Fredrickson, B.L. (2017). Being present and enjoying it: dispositional mindfulness and savouring the moment are distinct, interactive predictors of positive emotions and psychological health. *Mindfulness, 8*(5), 1280–1290.

Klimecki, O. and Singer, T. (2012). Empathic distress fatigue rather than compassion fatigue? Integrating findings from empathy research in psychology and social neuroscience. *Pathological Altruism,* 368–383.

Lee, J.H., Jung, H.K., Lee, G.G., Kim, H.Y., Park, S.G., and Woo, S.C. (2013). Effect of behavioural intervention using smartphone application for preoperative anxiety in pediatric patients. *Korean Journal of Anesthesiology, 65*(6), 508.

LeJeune, J. and Luoma, J.B. (2019). *Values in Therapy: A Clinician's Guide to Helping Clients Explore Values, Increase Psychological Flexibility, and Live a More Meaningful Life.* Oakland, CA: Context Press.

Maheux, A. and Price, M. (2016). The indirect effect of social support on post-trauma psychopathology via self-compassion. *Personality and Individual Differences, 88,* 102–107.

Margolis, H. and McCabe, P.P. (2006). Improving self-efficacy and motivation: what to do, what to say. *Intervention in School and Clinic, 41*(4), 218–227.

Markell, K.A. and Markell, M.A. (2013). *The Children Who Lived: Using Harry Potter and Other Fictional Characters to Help Grieving Children and Adolescents.* New York: Routledge.

Masuda, A., Feinstein, A.B., Wendell, J.W., and Sheehan, S.T. (2010). Cognitive defusion versus thought distraction: a clinical rationale, training, and experiential exercise in altering psychological impacts of negative self-referential thoughts. *Behavior Modification, 34*(6), 520–538.

McCracken, L.M. and Morley, S. (2014). The psychological flexibility model: a basis for integration and progress in psychological approaches to chronic pain management. *The Journal of Pain, 15*(3), 221–234.

McGonigal, J. (2015). *SuperBetter: A Revolutionary Approach to Getting Stronger, Happier, Braver, and More Resilient.* New York: Penguin Press.

McGrath, E.P. and Repetti, R.L. (2002). A longitudinal study of children's depressive symptoms, self-perceptions, and cognitive distortions about the self. *Journal of Abnormal Psychology, 111*(1), 77–87.

Melamed, S., Shirom, A., Toker, S., Berliner, S., and Shapira, I. (2006). Burnout and risk of cardiovascular disease: evidence, possible causal paths, and promising research directions. *Psychological Bulletin, 132*(3), 327–353.

Menadue, C.B. and Jacups, S. (2018). Who reads science fiction and fantasy, and how do they feel about science? Preliminary findings from an online survey. *SAGE Open, 8*(2), 2158244018780946.

Neff, K.D. and Dahm, K.A. (2015). 'Self-Compassion: What It Is, What It Does, and How It Relates to Mindfulness.' In B.D. Ostafin, M.D. Robinson, and D.P. Meier (eds) *Handbook of Mindfulness and Self-Regulation.* New York: Springer.

Neff, K. and Germer, C. (2018). *The Mindful Self-Compassion Workbook: A Proven Way to Accept Yourself, Build Inner Strength, and Thrive.* New York: The Guilford Press.

Øverup, C.S., McLean, E.A., Brunson, J.A., and Coffman, A.D. (2017). Belonging, burdensomeness, and self-compassion as mediators of the association between attachment and depression. *Journal of Social and Clinical Psychology, 36*(8), 675–703.

Park, C.L. and Ai, A.L. (2006). Meaning making and growth: new directions for research on survivors of trauma. *Journal of Loss and Trauma, 11*(5), 389–407.

Park, C.L., Riley, K.E., and Snyder, L.B. (2012). Meaning making coping, making sense, and post-traumatic growth following the 9/11 terrorist attacks. *The Journal of Positive Psychology, 7*(3), 198–207.

Peña, J. and Chen, M. (2017). With great power comes great responsibility: superhero primes and expansive poses influence prosocial behaviour after a motion-controlled game task. *Computers in Human Behavior, 76,* 378–385.

Pollard, C. and Kennedy, P. (2007). A longitudinal analysis of emotional impact, coping strategies and post-traumatic psychological growth following spinal cord injury: a 10-year review. *British Journal of Health Psychology, 12*(3), 347–362.

Prasad, S., Scarlet, J., and Prasadam, S.E. (under review). Psychology of Popular Media Effects of Superhero Therapy on Self-Compassion, Psychological inflexibility and Courage in Young Adults. Unpublished manuscript.

Reid, A.M., Garner, L.E., Van Kirk, N., Gironda, C. et al. (2017). How willing are you? Willingness as a predictor of change during treatment of adults with obsessive–compulsive disorder. *Depression and Anxiety, 34*(11), 1057–1064.

Roemer, L., Lee, J.K., Salters-Pedneault, K., Erisman, S.M., Orsillo, S.M., and Mennin, D.S. (2009). Mindfulness and emotion regulation difficulties in generalized anxiety disorder: preliminary evidence for independent and overlapping contributions. *Behavior Therapy, 40*(2), 142–154.

Rosenberg, R.S., Baughman, S.L., and Bailenson, J.N. (2013). Virtual superheroes: using superpowers in virtual reality to encourage prosocial behaviour. *PLoS ONE One, 8*(1), e55003.

Rosenberg, R.S. and Letamendi, A.M. (2013). Expressions of fandom: findings from a psychological survey of cosplay and costume wear. *Intensities: The Journal of Cult Media, 5,* 9–18.

Russoniello, C.V., O'Brien, K., and Parks, J.M. (2009). EEG, HRV and psychological correlates while playing Bejeweled II: a randomized controlled study. *Annual Review of Cybertherapy and Telemedicine, 7*(1), 189–192.

Russoniello, C.V., Fish, M., and O'Brien, K. (2013). The efficacy of casual videogame play in reducing clinical depression: a randomized controlled study. *Games for Health: Research, Development, and Clinical Applications, 2*(6), 341–346.

Scarlet, J. (2016). *Superhero Therapy: A Hero's Journey through Acceptance and Commitment Therapy.* London: Little, Brown Book Group.

Scarlet, J. (2017). *Harry Potter Therapy: An Unauthorized Self-Help Book from the Restricted Section.* Seattle, WA: CreateSpace.

Scarlet, J. (2020). *Supernatural Therapy: Hunting Your Internal Monsters IRL.* Seattle, WA: CreateSpace.

Sheline, Y.I., Barch, D.M., Price, J.L. *et al.* (2009). The default mode network and self-referential processes in depression. *Proceedings of the National Academy of Sciences, 106*(6), 1942–1947.

Sterling, M., Hendrikz, J., and Kenardy, J. (2011). Similar factors predict disability and posttraumatic stress disorder trajectories after whiplash injury. *Pain, 152*(6), 1272–1278.

Stern, S.C., Robbins, B., Black, J.E., and Barnes, J.L. (2019). What you read and what you believe: genre exposure and beliefs about relationships. *Psychology of Aesthetics, Creativity, and the Arts, 13*(4), 450–461.

Sutton-Smith, B. (1999). Evolving a consilience of play definitions: playfully. *Play and Culture Studies, 2,* 239–256.

Tarr, B., Launay, J., and Dunbar, R.I. (2016). Silent disco: dancing in synchrony leads to elevated pain thresholds and social closeness. *Evolution and Human Behavior, 37*(5), 343–349.

Tedeschi, R.G. and Calhoun, L.G. (1996). The Posttraumatic Growth Inventory: measuring the positive legacy of trauma. *Journal of Traumatic Stress, 9*(3), 455–471.

Thompson, B.L. and Waltz, J. (2008). Self-compassion and PTSD symptom severity. *Journal of Traumatic Stress: Official Publication of the International Society for Traumatic Stress Studies, 21*(6), 556–558.

Thompson, B.L. and Waltz, J. (2010). Mindfulness and experiential avoidance as predictors of posttraumatic stress disorder avoidance symptom severity. *Journal of Anxiety Disorders, 24*(4), 409–415.

Van Dam, N.T., Sheppard, S.C., Forsyth, J.P., and Earleywine, M. (2011). Self-compassion is a better predictor than mindfulness of symptom severity and quality of life in mixed anxiety and depression. *Journal of Anxiety Disorders, 25*(1), 123–130.

Vezzali, L., Stathi, S., Giovannini, D., Capozza, D., and Trifiletti, E. (2015). The greatest magic of Harry Potter: reducing prejudice. *Journal of Applied Social Psychology, 45*(2), 105–121.

Vinney, C. and Dill-Shackleford, K.E. (2018). Fan fiction as a vehicle for meaning making: eudaimonic appreciation, hedonic enjoyment, and other perspectives on fan engagement with television. *Psychology of Popular Media Culture, 7*(1), 18–32.

Waite, F., Knight, M.T., and Lee, D. (2015). Self-compassion and self-criticism in recovery in psychosis: an interpretative phenomenological analysis study. *Journal of Clinical Psychology, 71*(12), 1201–1217.

Wansink, B., Shimizu, M., and Camps, G. (2012). What would Batman eat?: priming children to make healthier fast food choices. *Pediatric Obesity, 7*(2), 121–123.

Weinstein, D., Launay, J., Pearce, E., Dunbar, R.I., and Stewart, L. (2016). Group music performance causes elevated pain thresholds and social bonding in small and large groups of singers. *Evolution and Human Behavior: Official Journal of the Human Behavior and Evolution Society, 37*(2), 152.

Wheeler, I. (2001). Parental bereavement: the crisis of meaning. *Death Studies, 25*(1), 51–66.

White, R.E. and Carlson, S.M. (2015). What would Batman do? Self-distancing improves executive function in young children. *Developmental Science, 19*(3), 419–426.

Xu, J. and Roberts, R.E. (2010). The power of positive emotions: it's a matter of life or death – subjective well-being and longevity over 28 years in a general population. *Health Psychology, 29*(1), 9–19.

Zeligman, M., Varney, M., Grad, R.I., and Huffstead, M. (2018). Posttraumatic growth in individuals with chronic illness: the role of social support and meaning making. *Journal of Counseling and Development, 96*(1), 53–63.

About the Author

Dr. Janina Scarlet is a licensed clinical psychologist, author, and a full-time geek. A Ukrainian-born refugee, she survived Chernobyl radiation and persecution. She immigrated to the United States at the age of 12 with her family and later, inspired by the X-Men, developed Superhero Therapy to help patients with anxiety, depression, and PTSD. Dr. Scarlet is the recipient of the Eleanor Roosevelt Human Rights Award by the United Nations Association for her work on Superhero Therapy. Her work has been featured on Yahoo, BBC, NPR, *The Sunday Times*, CNN, CW, ABC, Huffington Post, *The New York Times*, Forbes, Nerdist, BuzzFeed, and many other outlets. She currently works at the Center for Stress and Anxiety Management in San Diego.

She has authored *Superhero Therapy: A Hero's Journey through Acceptance and Commitment Therapy* (2016); *Harry Potter Therapy: An Unauthorized Self-Help Book from the Restricted Section* (2017); *Therapy Quest: An Interactive Journey through Acceptance and Commitment Therapy; Dark Agents, Book One: Violet and the Trial of Trauma* (2020); *Super-Women: Superhero Therapy for Women Battling Depression, Anxiety and Trauma* (2020); *Supernatural Therapy: Hunting Your Internal Monsters IRL* (2020), as well as numerous contributions to *Star Wars Psychology: Dark Side of the Mind* (Langley, 2015); *Star Trek Psychology: The Mental Frontier* (Langley, 2017); *Wonder Woman Psychology: Lassoing the Truth* (2017); *Supernatural Psychology: Roads Less Traveled* (2017), and many other books.

Index

Superhero Therapy Online Training Course
Janina Scarlet

£35.00 | $50.00 | ISBN 978 1 83997 071 9

Are you interested in using Superhero Therapy with your clients, but feel unsure where to start?

This series of eight bite-sized videos is the perfect introduction to Superhero Therapy, and will help you to incorporate the approach into your work with clients of all ages with anxiety and PTSD.

Covering everything from how clients can formulate an origin story to "gamifying" homework and more, these videos show how to incorporate popular culture into evidence-based approaches and create an effective treatment plan using Superhero Therapy. They are suitable as a standalone resource, or as an accompanying resource to the *Superhero Therapy for Anxiety and Trauma* book.

If you are a mental health professional looking for a creative and exciting way to help your clients, these videos are an ideal first step.